A Walk in the Lover's Garden

A personal meditation on the Song of Songs

Sue Aldridge

Onwards and Upwards Publishers

Berkeley House, 11 Nightingale Crescent, Leatherhead,
Surrey, KT24 6PD.
www.onwardsandupwards.org

Printed in the UK.

ISBN: 978-1-907509-80-3
Typeface: Sabon LT
Illustrator: Jackie Hutchinson
Graphic design: Leah-Maarit

Endorsements

Sue was an introvert, a deep thinker with a gift to communicate the transforming power of Jesus. She surrendered her life to Him totally and challenged me and many others to plunge deeper into a relationship with Him, to be completely open to Him, no matter what the cost. Sue loved to journal her journey. She communicated best in writing and would often tell her deepest thoughts, joys and struggles by letter. In the year 2000, Sue suffered a debilitating stroke that severely affected her speech and her mobility. In the ten years that remained of her life, Sue refused to be defeated by her disabilities and, with great difficulty and perseverance, completed what would turn out to be her life's work: her personal reflections on the Song of Songs. In these daily readings, encounter the Jesus she knew, the Lover of your soul. As you walk through the Lover's garden you will discover, as I did, that to journey with Sue is to be encouraged to keep walking, to be open to Jesus to make you whole – in body, mind and spirit.

Sue Hollywell
October 2014

If God were just an idea, the way to know God would be to think about God. If God were merely a force field, we could conduct an experiment to measure God's effects. But God is a person, and so to know God you have to have a relationship with Him. God is Love; God is the Eternal Lover, the One who wants to be the Supreme Love in our lives. So it is by means of imagination and intimacy, desire and delight, longing and fulfilment that we discover the Lover whose love never wavers nor dims. And only one like Sue, who knew through experience the ecstasy which overcomes all agony, can guide us as we journey into joy.

Dr David McIlroy
Barrister and Theologian
Associate Tutor, Spurgeon's College

This book is dedicated to a
wonderful friend, lover, wife,
mother and grandmother. May you
still rest in the Gardener's arms.

Also dedicated to my family – Joy
& Doug, Toby, and Madison
McIlroy; Faith – and to my special
friend Katrina Burton (Kat) for her
wonderful support and always
being there for me. Thanks!

Ron Aldridge

About the Author

Susan Aldridge (1952-2010) was a skilled teacher both in the church and in society. Already as a child, she wanted to teach in schools. However, at the age of sixteen, she suffered a 'sub-arrachnoid haemorrhage' and missed a term of her education. She was told that teaching was out of the question, she would have no children and she would be on medication for the rest of her life. However, a group of ladies in Datchet were praying... She attained the required A levels and entered teaching training college at Twickenham (despite a hockey accident just before her interview). During her first teacher training school visit Sue went to Basingstoke, where she sensed God's presence, became a Christian and was filled with the Holy Spirit.

Sue married Ron in August 1973 and began her teaching career in Slough, moving to Capel in 1975. Six years later, Sue and Ron decided to have children and were blessed with two daughters – Joy (born 30th April, 1981) and Faith (born 22nd July, 1989). Meanwhile, Sue continued teaching, eventually becoming head of a local school.

In 1996/7, Sue changed her career, working as the Sussex Baptist Association Administrator and Ladies' Leader. She began to preach locally and started the 'Free to be me' teachings with Hilary Malpass and other ladies. She served for two terms on the leadership of Trafalgar Road Baptist Church, where she was also leader of Parents & Toddlers and the Sunday school superintendent.

In 1999 she suffered a stroke and was in hospital for seven months. Just a couple of months after being discharged, she had a fit and was subsequently diagnosed an epileptic. However, Ron took early retirement from work, so that he could take Sue to her continued preaching engagements. In February 2010, it was discovered that Sue had cancer of the lower bowel and, despite treatment, the Father took her to be with him the same year.

Sue loved her family, church, walking and bird watching, but the greatest love she had was for God, with whom she enjoyed remarkable intimacy. Her journals reveal no sense of bitterness, only trust, and her life affected many people for good. She was determined, a fighter, a good friend to all, and God's servant.

Ron Aldridge
August 2013

Acknowledgements

I am grateful for the help and enthusiasm given by Sue's friends at Trafalgar Road Baptist Church, and to Sue Hollywell and Hilary Malpass, both Sue's 'soul mates' when she started writing this book.

Many thanks to Jackie Hutchinson for her wonderful illustrations. And also to Faith in helping me with this book.

Ron Aldridge
August 2013

Publisher's Preface

This book of daily meditations is based on a series of notes made by Sue Aldridge during the later years of her life. The original notes consisted of historical, cultural and textual research, questions, allegorical and personal application, prayers and responses from God. These have been organized and edited into 150 daily readings, enabling readers to work systematically through the Song of Solomon and apply it to their own lives and experiences. Sue explains:

> ...God has called me often to meditate in Song of Songs; sometimes to learn about what it is to be in love with Him and to have Him in love with me, sometimes to speak into a current situation ... Often Jesus has spoken directly into my current situation or into my present relationships through Song of Songs, and so you will be sharing with me some of the highs and lows of everyday life. I trust that you will not find this shifting of focus from the story to real life too disconcerting but will find that Jesus reveals Himself to you as Lover of your soul in the everyday scenes of life that you live with Him.

The daily notes written by Sue are followed by thoughts for prayer and contemplation. These have been written partly by Sue and partly by the book's editor.

Foreword by Bill McIlroy

I watched as the nurse checked Sue's vital signs. She gave no reply to her name, no movement in her eyes, no reflex in her hands, feet or knees; nothing indicated she was still with us except a few wavy lines on the monitors by her bed. Sue remained there in Intensive Care through many weeks and frequent trips to theatre to have fluid drained from her infected brain. The fact that she was able subsequently to write this book is a miracle – the combination of God's grace and the love and insistent prayers of her friends.

This series of reflections on the Song of Songs therefore comes from a person who in 2000 lay for a while at heaven's gate and then returned. Its intimacy, personal candour and spiritual longing reads like someone who has been excited by the aroma of heaven, just as returning sailors of old could smell the land before they saw it. It seems appropriate that this series of reflections has been edited into just 150 days because humanly speaking the life of this former deputy head teacher and popular Christian seminar leader was cut short. In this book her ministry continues.

If you come casually to these pages you may struggle with their intensity and intimacy, but if you are prepared to sit with this allegory and allow Sue's thoughts to quicken your understanding of the love relationship you have with Jesus then you will be well rewarded. Perhaps, like me, you will find yourself turning again to the Bible thirsty for the Holy Spirit to reveal more to you and to 'hear the waterfall of love'.

Bill McIlroy
East Surrey District Minister,
Former Pastor of Trafalgar Road Baptist Church, Horsham

Introduction

To write a book that will contain so much of my soul seems suicidal. Those close to me tell me my soul is beautiful and that you would be blessed by catching a glimpse of it. I find that impossible to believe – for all I see is the wretchedness that is me. I reason, however, that even if you only see my wretchedness you may be encouraged by my honest journey to believe that God cares intimately for you, and I hope you'll see that I know He loves me intimately.

By reason of the time that it takes to write these words and get them translated into print and off into your hands, I will have changed even now as these words enter your heart. The Christian journey is one that is always on the move; we are either growing or dying. Perchance we will meet. Don't be surprised if I've changed from how you receive me in these words. I hope we'll both be glad and surprised by the ways Jesus has changed us both to be more like Him. This is no dialogue but rather a three-way process – you, me and Jesus – souls touching through the words on the page.

As I've read Song of Songs, so the same three-way transformation has taken place. Jesus, Solomon and I (Wow! What lofty company I've shared!) have joined souls, and the Holy Spirit, Scripture's author, has opened all three souls to touch and bring about transformation in me.

Let's enter this journey of discovery breathless with anticipation of each new revelation of Jesus, Lover of our souls. Rejoice with me for those who have gifted me their souls to explore; for what I read and know on the page, and in the intimate place with Jesus alone, has to be risked in the precious souls of others as we journey through life's experiences. Such rare sacrifice is priceless.

As we turn the pages of our Bible to Song of Songs we realise what a small portion of Scripture it is – how easily we overshoot as we fly past Psalms, Proverbs and headlong on into the Major Prophets. However, this book is the entrance to a depth of relationship with Jesus that may not be found in any other book contained in Scripture. So rest a while before God and whisper a heart prayer of submission to the Holy Spirit, a prayer that touches

11

the Father's heart and releases you to receive the revelation of Jesus that the Holy Spirit inspired the Word's authors to pen. The name of Jesus is powerful to conquer strongholds and it is tender to melt hearts. Through His interpretation, Jesus will become a reality in your complete and human experience, for this Son of God is also fully man.

I wish it were in my power to grant complete satisfaction upon discovering Jesus as Lover of your soul. That is not mine to grant. But I can confidently point to Him and say, with Paul, "...for I have learned to be content whatever the circumstances" (Philippians 4:6, NIV), for my knowledge and experience of His faithfulness give me a certain hope of satisfaction beyond my wildest imaginings. In this life I continue to have unearthed the mysteries that fire my entire being. I am choosing to walk into the pain of disappointment to seek out the joy for which my soul pants. I hear the waterfall of Love and I hold its melody in even the deepest turmoil.

DAY 1

Song of Songs 1:1 (NIV)
Solomon's Song of Songs

- Solomon – the wise king, the master builder, one who worked to plans and fulfilled his father's commands.
- Solomon – revered and feared. Yet one who poured out his words in a song to reveal a longing so deep that so much remains unfathomable.
- Solomon – who got it so right with his wise, God-given judgments and who got it so wrong with his fallen, human judgment. One who fell yet knew there was compassion in God's heart.

The song is *the* Song of Songs. For Solomon, it's the epitome of songs, a self-revelation that opens his soul for the world to see, but intended solely for the ears, eyes, heart and soul of the Beloved.

- Solomon – forerunner of Jesus!
- Solomon – totally man and walking close to God!
- Jesus – totally man and totally God!

To read this as Jesus' Song of Songs opens the door to us to explore the surface of the deep and beyond, of Jesus' love for us, both collectively as His Bride and individually as those beloved of God.

Such is the extent of His love (Ephesians 3:20) that one person's exploration reveals just a fraction of the truth. I give you my fraction, so that added with yours we may experience the mathematics of God that expands our minds and experience to believe there is more. God multiplies in abundance; as we give away what I know, He will return it so lavishly to us because His presence is always greater than our limited imagination.

Prayer & Contemplation: *What do you already know about Jesus' love for you? Has that knowledge become a daily experience for you? What aspect of His love would you like to understand better?*

DAY 2

Song of Songs 1:2a (KJV)
Let Him kiss me with the kisses of His mouth...

It would be considered audacious to kiss an earthly king, but here is the Beloved, asking for the King of Kings to kiss her. Such is the tenderness of Jesus, and His desire to be tenderly intimate, that He will kiss us. As we read through Song of Songs we see that complete intimacy is reached, and just as with courting couples today, it begins with the longing to be close enough to kiss. Scripture talks of a *holy* kiss, and we might call to mind kissing the Pope's hand, a formal bowing to authority. But that is not what kissing Jesus means. Bowing to his authority has its place as we acknowledge His authority, sovereignty and lordship over us. To attempt to enter into the deep intimate place without first acknowledging Jesus as all of these is folly indeed. We hold in tension the relationships we have with Jesus and need to be cautious that we don't go overboard in any direction. Not that if we do, He will not throw us a lifebelt – that's what Grace is all about!

When Jesus kisses me, He kisses *me* – my soul, that bit of me which is a mystery to be discovered. His kiss evokes a response in my soul and arouses every nerve ending and sinew. The longing to be kissed again like that overwhelms, and I often choose instead to follow after earthly replicas which satisfy fleetingly – or I can choose to remain in the pain of longing that He will return and kiss my soul again. Just as the kiss of life to a drowned body restores life, so this Kiss of Life to my drained soul restores life in abundance.

Prayer & Contemplation: *What is your image of Jesus? Can you perceive him as one who wants to be close and intimate? Are you willing to receive his kisses?*

DAY 3

Song of Songs 1:2b (NASB)
...for your love is better than wine.

Being a medical teetotaller this verse is difficult for me to understand. Although I did sample alcohol as a young teenager, all I can remember is the bitter taste and perhaps the tingle of forbiddenness. Never having been inebriated I cannot fathom whether the sensations are more or less pleasing than love. However I can say that my experience of receiving Jesus' love is so totally captivating that it makes every nerve ending tingle; I suspect that even the effect of alcohol could not match that! The wonderful thing about love by comparison with alcohol is that there is no painful hangover – although there *is* a deep, deep longing to experience it again... and that longing can be painful. There is no physical headache, fuzzy tongue etc. as there is from the legacy of drink, but there are deep pains of emotional hunger as Jesus' love awakens longings in our soul which bring us alive and tell us, "This is what life and living is all about." I could at this point break into as full a description as I can muster of the feelings of 'aliveness' that an encounter with the Lover of my soul brings, but to do that would only lead to repetition later. So I offer you a taster of 'aliveness' to draw you into further exploration of ourselves and our Lover as we wander through the ensuing scriptures.

Prayer & Contemplation: *Ponder a few of the moments in life that have brought this overwhelming sense of wellbeing to the surface. What prompted those feelings? Can you see and feel God in the circumstances? If you can, ask Him to reveal why He was there and what He was showing you. If you can't, ask Him to reveal Himself to you.*

DAY 4

Song of Songs 1:3 (NIV)
Pleasing is the fragrance of your perfumes; your name is like perfume poured out. No wonder the young women love you!

Having described the Lover with one of her senses – her taste – the Beloved now uses another – her sense of smell. She may well be describing a physical perfume that has been applied externally – especially as she could be talking about the King. But I also expect she's talking about his natural physical aroma.

A perfume – like wine – touches the senses and stimulates the hormones. It brings inner physical sensations – either of immense pleasure (which would stimulate her entire being) or of something totally noxious (which would stimulate a different set of responses and an equal physical reaction). As she uses the word 'pleasing' we know that she intends the former and not the latter. I recognise many times when the presence of Jesus has provoked physical responses in my body as would the familiar perfume of someone beloved.

Prayer & Contemplation:

"Lord, there is a sense of welcome and belonging when there is a familiar perfume – a wellbeing that says, "This is safe; this is comfortable; this is where I belong." I realise how little I've experienced of Your perfume of late. I've sorrowed at the realisation but rejoice that You've shown the way back – because the mention of Your Name is perfume. In the stillness I begin to sense the aroma of Your presence – not in great, strong, over-powering fragrance but in gentle wafts as they pass my nose. You are indeed sweet. You are gentle, gracious and generous – grace personified. I rest – still – before You and ponder other fragrances that touch me. Some – like newly mown grass, baby powder, my husband's deodorant, my soul-mate's house – rise in my memory, and I am at peace, secure in these friendly, familiar fragrances. Some – like the smell of cooking cabbage or of the 'many bodies with sweaty plimsolls' odour of school – make me recoil. These are all familiar aromas but each has its own set of physical and emotional responses. Still, the aroma of You is the hope of Life on the one hand but the stench of death for those who choose not to meet with you."

DAY 5

Song of Songs 1:3b (RSV)
...therefore the maidens love you.

The pleasing fragrance of the Lover and His name bring forth this response from the Beloved. The name of the Beloved would have been hugely significant in Bible times, given to reflect character and potential – something we find hard to grasp nowadays when often names are given for no particular reason or because of 'hero worship'. I wonder if the maidens can be likened to the whole church of Jesus, the Bride of Christ; those who truly meet Jesus fall in love with Him not because of outward beauty but because of the alluring fragrance of His personality, unlike anything found in other humans. Maybe if I could take all the best human bits of all the people I know I could create in some small measure a human that matched Jesus, but I still think what I create would fall so far short of the reality of who Jesus is. In relationship I connect with the parts of another's character that touch me. Often they will give me so little that it's only that little that I can relate to. Sometimes, by grace and godly insight, I can see beyond the way someone presents themself to me, and God reveals potential in them.

> *Behind men's grumpiest poses and most puzzling defence mechanisms, behind their arrogance and airs, behind their silence, sneers and curses, Jesus saw little children who hadn't been loved enough and who had ceased growing because someone had ceased believing in them.[1]*

That excites me and fills me with hope, and I wonder if the person I am talking to knows that it is in them! Sometimes it's 'yes, they do', for in the discussion they share that bit of who they are. Sometimes, despite me repeatedly saying who they are, they seem unable to accept that what I describe could possibly be them. I understand that; sometimes we stand so close to our rubbish heap that we can't see the flowers in the garden. Jesus grows in arid, dark, dank places as well as in beautiful, light and airy places. Perfume can penetrate darkness. I may not be able to see my husband, I may not be able to hear him,

---

[1] *'The Signature of Jesus'*, Brennan Manning; published by Random House.

nor touch him – but sometimes I know he's there; I can smell his fragrance. So it is with Jesus; even when the aroma He brings to our noses is putrid because He is reflecting our darker sides, there is still the perfume of Love mingled in. We dare to follow Love by wading through the putrefying rubbish of our lives which, in the confronting, is transformed by Jesus. No wonder the maidens love Him!

Prayer & Contemplation: *Tell Jesus what you love about His fragrance, His personality. Is there someone else whom you could encourage by telling them about the good God has placed in them?*

Day 6

Song of Songs 1:4a (NLT)
Take me with you; come, let's run!

When God calls me to walk through the revolting side of who I have become and I see my ugliness and taste my bitterness... I find I long to be away from all of this. The world ensnares and encroaches; it is a constant battle against the evil side of my nature, and I would rather be out of this battle! It becomes wearisome, especially when the same foes have to be beaten again and again! Heaven can't come fast enough!

Prayer & Contemplation: *Tell Jesus how you feel about His calling to run together. Perhaps the prayer below echoes your feelings too.*

> *"Lord, to see You in Your glory rather than to have You see me in my degradation becomes an ever-increasing heart-cry. But if I were in glory, although I would be free, I would be leaving others behind still bound. I recognise the reality of the need to stay in this world and not be of it, even though sometimes self would rather flee the battlefield and be nurtured in heaven."*

DAY 7

Song of Songs 1:4b (KJV)
...the king hath brought me into his chambers...

To ponder the King's chambers! Now, what would they be like? Living where I did I was privileged to regularly visit the 'King's chambers' (or at least the State Apartments) at Windsor Castle. All the grandiose adjectives imaginable are applicable. Reading Scripture we get glimpses of Heaven that far outweigh any human splendour, Windsor Castle included! But I suspect that when we get to Heaven we will be too transfixed by the King to really absorb what the surroundings are like! Just because we're in Heaven the fragrance of His perfume will not diminish or cease; it is far more likely to intensify to the extent that it pervades every atom of our being. There are those who say when we get to Heaven we'll spend all of our time flat on our faces; I'm not so sure. At the judgement we may well fall down and worship but I don't believe that we'll be denied Jesus' eyes, and if we're to look into His eyes then we must have our faces turned toward Him!

Maybe that's why the Beloved is so eager to be brought into the King's chambers; the longing to be soaked in His perfume and gaze into His eyes is all-consuming. Will we be allowed to be alone with the King? I hope so! Currently, we are bound by the dimensions of time and space; as Heaven is beyond these, will it be possible for us all to always be alone with Him and gaze into His eyes? Wouldn't that be wonderful? Will it be contentment at just one moment to have one glimpse into the Saviour's soul? Can that glimpse be eternal? In my spirit I have gazed into my Lover's eyes, and that gaze has been enough to keep me searching for His eyes again. The giving of such a love-gift frees me to be who I am, but in the freedom the longing draws me after more.

Prayer & Contemplation: *Imagine Jesus bringing you into His chambers and gazing lovingly into your eyes. Remain in that place with him for a while. Don't hurry away! Tell Him what is on your heart, and listen to His reply.*

DAY 8

Song of Songs 1:4c (NIV)
<u>Friends</u> *We rejoice and delight in you; we will praise your love more than wine.*

I don't know if the Beloved's friends were like mine or if they were more like Job's comforters! They appear in this verse to be more like mine and want to share the Beloved's delight. It is painful to have joy and delight to share and not have those closest to you to be able to share it with. I remember being at a conference, surrounded by people – but they were strangers or acquaintances and could not know how deeply significant and personal many of the things I received from God were! Acquaintances would not have known the depth of my joy, or the freedom of my release, or the surge of acceptance and confirmation, because they did not know me and had not journeyed through my struggles – nor I theirs! It would have been wonderful to have had my friends there with me, for them to taste my delight (definitely greater than wine) as it happened.

Reporting it in hindsight, they still share it deeply, but I grieve the loss of immediacy, intimacy and the possibility of them receiving from a common experience. "Look! See!" is so much more memory-enhancing than "I wish you could have looked!" It seems like there had been potential for memories to have been made but they couldn't be – so for practical reasons I seem to have been denied greater joy. It might sound churlish and greedy for us to think this way, but in reality it's a longing that maybe one day such an opportunity will be afforded to us.

Prayer & Contemplation: *Are there times you have wished there had been close friends with you to share special moments? Thank God for the friends he has given you, and express to Him your desire to share more of your life with them.*

> *"Lord, I know what it is like to have friends rejoice with me, and I know what it is to rejoice with friends. Sometimes I've felt the pangs of not being able to share the delights I've found in You because my friends haven't been there with me. Shared experiences mean so much!"*

DAY 9

Song of Songs 1:4c (NIV)
Friends We rejoice and delight in you; we will praise your love more than wine.

The Beloved's friends seem to be present to share much of the Beloved's delight. We can never share totally because we are uniquely different with different experiences of life, but we understand far more fully when we are sharing the experience in time rather than in the reporting.

I am so thankful that I have been blessed with two beautiful, loving, tenacious, understanding, Jesus-filled soul-mates, who express their sorrow and delights and who share mine. Sometimes my eyes sparkle in response as they describe experiences akin to my own. Yet other times my eyes sparkle with their joy but my soul is not yet prepared by experience to receive what they share. There is pain in that, but a longing too – it leads me to want to find God in such a way. I know that when I share an experience that, as of yet, is beyond them, they too walk in the same pain of longing. We receive by faith the gift given, are jealous to receive the same (but not in a consuming way) and are prepared to learn that such knowledge may not be for us yet, or may never be for us. We rejoice in each other's treasure; we're blessed in the sharing of it, and we wonder!

Prayer & Contemplation: *What do the lives of your friends reveal about God that you have yet to experience? Seek Him for a deeper relationship with him in these areas. Ask Him show anything that stands in the way.*

> *"Lord, wine intoxicates and dulls the human senses, often leaving us regretting our over-imbibing. You, on the other hand, bring us alive in all our senses, and the only regrets we're left with are that we've left it so long to search for You or that we were not sufficiently ready to receive more of You."*

DAY 10

Song of Songs 1:4d (NLT)
How right they are to adore you.

I realise that my spirit is with God, for I'll find a song on my lips and be humming or whistling or rehearsing the words inwardly whilst all of my other faculties are elsewhere engaged. Often I will wake up with songs or Scripture feeding my mind. I can be well into an activity before I realise, by tuning in, exactly what my subconscious mind is doing. That blesses me and encourages me for I know that I am feeding on the finest of fruits. Sadly those times are not as often as I would like, and when my conscious mind tunes in to what is under the surface I find myself dwelling on negatives, either about me or about others or about situations. It is getting better – my mind is being transformed – but frustration at the tardiness of the process often thwarts the healing!

Prayer & Contemplation: *How can you live your life with a greater level of daily adoration of God?*

> *"Lord, I wonder how far short I fall from really adoring You. The world presses in, often with very godly demands, and my outward focus is definitely turned away from You. But where is my inner focus? Do I adore You in spirit, even when my mind and body are focused elsewhere? I think that the answer to that must be 'sometimes'. I hope it is more often than I realise."*

DAY 11

Song of Songs 1:5a (NIV)
Dark I am, yet lovely, daughters of Jerusalem...

The Beloved refers to her skin being dark but lovely. Different does not equal wrong; it equals different! We become more different the further we walk into God's Light... and the longer we remain there. Just as the physical sun darkens the skin and makes the individual stand out from those who've been in the shadows, so the spiritual Son transforms our spirits and makes us stand out from those who have lived in the shadows – even in the church.

Prayer & Contemplation: Are the aspects of whom God has made you that you do not appreciate? Do you wish to be more like others around you? Ask God to show you how he sees you. Ask Him to use those aspects of who you are in His perfect plan for your life – and for others.

"Lord, I hear You whisper that even though I perceive my self-nature to be dark, You see me as lovely. You will enable me to make the choices that bring me into the light so that the darkness, even though it's visible to all, may be seen as beautiful, lovely because You are transforming my darkness into light.

For the Beloved there is a reason for her darkness; for me too there are reasons why I am so dark. As I let You tend me there is healing for my darkness... but it's only found in the light.

As I feast my eyes on the beauty of Your creation, so you are feasting Your eyes on me. My darkness is nothing to be ashamed of; neither is Your light to me. If I am stared at (or if I perceive I am stared at) it is not a stare of humiliation or disgust; it's a stare of wonder, of noticing the difference."

DAY 12

Song of Songs 1:5b-6a (NASB)
...like the tents of Kedar, like the curtains of Solomon. Do not stare at me because I am swarthy.

Having stated that she is dark yet lovely, in speaking to the daughters of Jerusalem, the Beloved then gives two descriptive pictures of her darkness: the tents of Kedar and the tent curtains of Solomon. Tents are moveable homes, and we are often encouraged to extend the borders of our tents (Isaiah 54:2,3), yet I sense there is something particular about why these two types of tent are mentioned. They obviously describe the Beloved's darkness. When I'm made aware of the darkness of who I am, I don't want anyone to look at me, let alone My Lover... even I don't want to look at myself!

Prayer & Contemplation: *Do you find it hard to receive Jesus' love because of your darkness or sinfulness? Thank Him now that He has carried all this on the cross and can receive you as spotless and shining. Thank Him that He has made the first step towards you.*

"Evil is always described as black and dark, whilst truth is described as white and light. Yet even in the darkness of my depravity and sinfulness I still find You; shafts of Light break in and reveal the dancing colour of Light shining through gemstones.[2]"

---

[2] Isaiah 45:3

DAY 13

Song of Songs 1:6b (NASB)
My mother's sons were angry with me; they made me caretaker of the vineyards...

One of the thoughts that has been burning in my heart of late is that I should not just hold what I am given in open hands but actually choose to give it away.

I identify with the Beloved's frustration at tending her mother's sons' vineyards, for my understanding is that they have used and abused the vineyard for self-gratification whereas the Beloved would have used them for the good of others, for the glory of the Lover. Does she fear that even if she tended her own vineyard that her 'brothers' would abuse that too? I find that echoes deep in me, sounding alarm bells.

Prayer & Contemplation: *Have you neglected your vineyard? Have you been forced to look after the vineyards of others? Have you chosen to look after others' vineyards rather than your own? If you have, do you trust Jesus to tend yours? Or do you fear that what God has given you will be abused? Tell Him about this in prayer.*

DAY 14

Song of Songs 1:6b (NASB)
My mother's sons were angry with me; they made me caretaker of the vineyards...

Once day I shared my fear of abuse with Jesus: "There is a fear here, Lord. If I walk through this door of hope, will I find the treasure given abused? As that treasure I give is me, will I be abused? Having been abused I find that thought abhorrent; I feel the need to avoid that course of action at all costs. How can You ask me to risk the annihilation of the beauty You've placed in me?"

He replied, "I can ask you because you are Mine and so is your beauty. You understand that the only way Jesus could transform this sick, fallen and corrupt world was to give His all. The only way He will continue to do this work of transformation is to continue to give His all. He is in you. He loves you and will not ask you to do that which He has not already done himself and equipped you for.

"I will give you back your own vineyard. I will drink the wine of your vineyard in My Kingdom as I promised the Disciples. Like them you are called, you are sent out. You will tend other vineyards; some you will tend joyfully, some you will tend obediently, some you will tend fearfully – *but I am* with you.

"Just as you came out of Egypt, so you will bring many others with you. Look and see! They follow you in triumphal procession as you follow Me. You must keep following Me so that they may follow; there will be others who take the lead and then you must cheer them on and shout encouragement. Even in the face of insider persecution you must keep giving away. Give Me away! Give Me away!

"The Beloved was made to tend others' vineyards. It will feel like you are made to do the same. Recognise that you have a choice. Hear My Voice and follow Me into those vineyards. From your perspective it may feel and appear hopeless; the divine perspective is that if there is sap in the roots there is always potential for harvest!"

I wonder why the mother's sons were angry with the Beloved and what influence they had that enabled them to make her take care of their vineyards. Is she young and unable to realise that she may have a choice in the matter? Is she by tradition expected to do this and so thinks there is no choice? Is it that, as a female, she must bow to the males' demands? Is she dark from tending the vineyards of others or dark because of her neglect? Was she darkened by the sun and then made to tend the vineyard; could this be a form of punishment for slothfulness? We don't know; but whatever and however, her darkness is of great shame to her. Staring must have felt like humiliation so often – yet in the Lover is One who stares in loving disbelief and adoration!

How sad it is that the Beloved feels herself unworthy and unfruitful! As she's been working in others' vineyards, she hasn't been totally unfruitful for we must presume that their vineyards bore fruit. However, bearing fruit for others to get the credit leaves us feeling used and abused – worthless in ourselves, particularly when we perceive no personal choice in the matter. When we have *chosen* to work for another, giving our toil as a love-gift, then our worth is enhanced by the credit the others receive. However, this doesn't seem to be the case here.

Prayer & Contemplation: *How can you show appreciation and gratitude towards those people God has placed around you?*

> *"The more I ponder these verses and listen to all You're saying in so many arenas, I hear time and again the call to deep relationship with You, leading to personal holiness and growing from seeds planted by You, a deepening call to real relationship with those my life touches – Christian and non-Christian alike! I hear in the Beloved's voice a heart-cry for relationship, to be known beyond her outward appearance and her practical abilities in viticulture!"*

DAY 15

Song of Songs 1:6c
... my own vineyard I had to neglect.

I wonder how the Beloved said this. What was the emotion in her voice as she spoke? Sadness, longing, wistfulness? Anger, rebellion, rejection, revenge? Sorrow, fear, humiliation? These few words can be spoken in so many ways, each revealing the state of the soul and the focus of the heart. What would her hands have been doing? Thrown up in horror? Hiding her face in shame? Pointing the finger accusingly? Whichever, this statement reveals much about her current state, her self-worth, her sense of security, her emptiness where love is concerned – *real* love, deep unconditional love! We will see such a difference between her current emptiness and her later fullness, when she describes the Lover and the strong passions that he arouses in her.

Each new healing, each 'coming out of Egypt', each release from slavery, will cause us to re-evaluate our whole life. Wouldn't it be great if 'coming out of Egypt' could be one big exodus just like for the children of Israel? Probably not... It would probably be just as difficult as it was for them. Being free from slavery left an aching void, and they made so many wrong choices trying to fill it. So if I picture each child coming out of Egypt as a victory then I can begin to conceive the big picture of all of me coming out of slavery. Each fresh skirmish won is like another child crossing the Red Sea.

It takes only a little neglect for the fruit of the vineyards to begin to reveal that neglect. The greater the neglect, the poorer the fruit will be. So when I neglect my Lover and our relationship together, the fruit of my life is of a much poorer quality. Those who are used to picking the richest of fruit will soon notice the difference. Despite the darkness of the Beloved's shame, the poor quality of her fruit, the overgrown state of her vineyard and her confession of that state, the Lover does not cast her aside nor overlook her; instead, as we find later, the Lover builds her up with the description He gives.

Prayer & Contemplation: *Have you neglected the vineyard of your relationship with Jesus? He does not cast you aside! Come back to Him in prayer today. He is waiting!*

DAY 16

Song of Songs 1:7 (KJV)
Tell me, O you whom my soul loves, where do you pasture your flock, where do you make it lie down at noon? For why should I be like one who veils herself beside the flocks of your companions?

I don't believe that the Beloved wants to find the Lover's flocks so that she can tend them, although I suspect that would be a delight if she were asked. She describes the flocks as grazing and resting – both things that sheep can do unsupervised! No, here is the Beloved laying bare her desire: she no longer wishes to be veiled and hidden from Him nor from His friends. She is saying, "Know me! I am more than a dark-skinned girl. I am more than an outcast of society. I am more than a child-bearing machine. I am more than a toy, a conquest to parade before friends. I am *me*, and I long to be revealed completely."

The veil is a symbol of servitude, of belonging to another. How we hide behind our veils! How sad it is that so few, if any, really know us! The greater sadness is personal, for not being known leaves us not completely knowing ourselves. I could regularly weep for the might-have-beens and the if-onlys, but if I did that too often I'd miss the what-is and thereby be left with even greater melancholy!

In the heat of the midday sun, where would the One who tends the sheep be? At rest, by the water, feeding Himself; the Beloved is surely after finding the heart of the Lover, to know Him in His relaxed state and not in His official capacity. I wonder what she hopes she will find. As things unfold, I suspect what she finds out about the Lover (and perhaps more importantly, about herself) is beyond imagining; such is the descriptive poetic imagery that we shall enter and enjoy.

Prayer & Contemplation: Can you identify veils that you hide behind? How about in your relationship with God? Ask Him today to help you remove the veils and begin to shine with the glory and beauty He has placed within you.

Day 17

Song of Songs 1:8a (NIV)
Friends If you do not know, most beautiful of women...

How fortunate the Beloved is to have such affirming friends! The Beloved's question in verse 7 was rhetorically addressed to the Lover. How easy it would have been for those around her to have mocked or ridiculed. For me, the answer they gave was obvious and simple. They could have delivered it as a perfect put-down or to puff out their own chests. But they didn't! I'm sure they would not have addressed her as "most beautiful of women" if they were intent on self-righteousness and other-undermining!

What it is to hear words of affirmation – particularly from those who know us well! It is so easy to take those closest to us for granted. We understand that it is good to praise, but somehow our praises often get used up on those furthest away from us or for those we feel threatened by or those we view as superior to us. We ignore praising our loved ones at our peril, for from them is where we are most likely to receive the praise we need to flourish. If we don't praise and affirm then they are less likely to praise and affirm – and not necessarily out of malice or neglect but from a base of not perceiving themselves to be praiseworthy people. It becomes a case of *can't* praise not *won't* praise – because they no longer have the wherewithal! We love so much more easily and readily when we feel ourselves loved.

So it must be that the Beloved, shamed by her dark skin, is affirmed and encouraged so that her shame is destroyed in the flood of love she receives. In receiving love she is enabled to believe that she has love worthy to give her Lover. The Apostle John says:

1 John 4:19
We love because He first loved us.

How I need to constantly open myself to receive the love Jesus has for me! He loves me directly and intimately as I am quiet and still before Him. He loves me indirectly through others, who become to me His arms, His legs, His compassion, even His eyes. He even loves me through my activity as I hear His "Well done!" as I plough on through.

How we need friends like this – to love us with Jesus' love; to affirm us, our value, our uniqueness! Words are so important; they have the power to grow or to destroy. We must use them wisely, to show us the way to Jesus. So often we get so close to a problem that we lose sight of Him! The problem blocks our way and we see no route out! What joy to have friends who come alongside, bring perspective and show us where to place our next step!

Prayer & Contemplation: *To whom you can be a true friend today? Take the opportunity to speak words of encouragement and affirmation.*

DAY 18

Song of Songs 1:8a (NASB)
If you yourself do not know, most beautiful among women, go forth on the trail of the flock and pasture your young goats by the tents of the shepherds.

I used to keep myself to myself. No-one ever got near enough to show me Jesus or to show me the way. I arrogantly believed I could do this by myself! How poor I became! Yet God saw my impoverished state and sent persistent folk to be my friends, who sacrificed their own comfort for my sake, took me firmly by the hand (or as firmly as I would allow) and showed me Jesus. Such a love-gift is overwhelming!

Christ is in me, my hope of glory.
Christ is in me, my hope of glory.
Christ is in me, my hope of glory.
Christ is in me, my hope of glory.
Christ is in me, my hope of glory.
Christ is in me, my hope of glory.
Christ is in me, my hope of glory.
Christ is in me, my hope of glory.
I am not hopeless.

As Christ is in me, I am everything to You!
As Christ is in me, I can enjoy being everything to You!
As Christ is in me, You enjoy being everything to me!

The Beloved missed the Lover intensely. She longed after Him, even just a small part of Him. She dared to open up her feelings to her friends, to ask her questions out loud. And she found no humiliation – just love, acceptance, delight and direction. Her friends pointed the way! And she heard the Lover's song – lyrics that described how He felt about her and the impact she had on Him.

Having bemoaned the darkness of her skin, her friends call her the most beautiful of women! Either they don't see the dark skin but see beneath to the character and reality of who the Beloved is, or they consider the darkness of skin something beautiful. Either way the affirmation still flows.

Once, when I was with one of my closest friends, she didn't feel very beautiful; she was feeling a failure and somewhat depressed. I wished she could have sat where I was sitting and looked at herself with my eyes! I could see beyond the 'failed' label to the beauty of the winsomeness of her soul coming to terms with the longing in her soul that was proving to be so elusive. I knew there would come a point of surrender, just as it did for the Beloved. Time would tell when that would be, but as her friend I would wait patiently, pray powerfully, love tenderly, and keep telling her of the beauty I could see.

When we live in constant affirmation we will grow to become what others see in us. (That works the other way round, of course! When we live with constant criticism either from ourselves or others, we will live like that too!)

Are the tracks of the sheep obvious? What path do they take? Won't they be confused with the tracks of other sheep? Probably (especially the difficult ones) but it will be possible to find the right path! Sometimes the sheep's tracks are worldly. Isaiah describes us as sheep that have gone astray.[3] But, as John reminds us, we follow the Good Shepherd![4] He will know us by name and call us repeatedly.

Prayer & Contemplation: Do you keep yourself to yourself, or can you open up your feelings to your friends? Talk to Jesus about this!

> *"Lord, when we have loved ones, they know our new name too! When they speak it often we are more confident and move off following the tracks. When we seldom hear it we become insecure and may well stay where we are and bleat! How we have to use all our senses, especially common sense, to determine which set of tracks to follow!"*

---

[3] Isaiah 53:6
[4] John 10:14

DAY 19

Song of Songs 1:8a (NASB)
If you yourself do not know, most beautiful among women, go forth on the trail of the flock and pasture your young goats by the tents of the shepherds.

Is the Lover the shepherd? Or are these, the Lover's sheep, tended by a shepherd? It probably doesn't matter for somewhere their tracks will lead to the Lover. Sometimes we hear the shepherd's voice clearly and our Lover is the shepherd. Sometimes we don't hear at all well and we need other shepherds to speak to us, tend us and lead us to the Lover. Either way we get there through persistence. To choose one above the other may leave us missing out!

I wonder if it is significance that the Beloved had goats and the Lover had sheep. When Jesus talked about Judgment Day in Matthew 25:32, he said that the sheep and the goats would be separated. He implied that the sheep would be acceptable but not the goats. Maybe the friends considered the Beloved to be similarly 'unacceptable'.

Did the Beloved not only tend the vineyards – a full time job – but have to tend the goats too? They are called "your" young goats – is that hers as a possession? Or hers as yet another duty? Even if they were hers as a possession, if she had to tend the vineyard and look after the goats that really didn't leave her much time for anything else! No wonder she was desperate for human relationship! Reflecting back it appears that she had little opportunity to relate to anyone. Her mother's sons were angry with her – no real relationship there. Her mother did nothing to step in – no real relationship there. No mention of her father – but, as a daughter, tradition would decree no opportunity for relationship there. Thank God for friends, the only people who appear to be for her! (Other than the Lover, that is!)

How symptomatic all this is of so many family relationships – each individual seeking their own good irrespective of the effect on other members of the family – when family is the one place where we should feel safe, secure, valued and unconditionally loved!

Prayer & Contemplation: Do you keep yourself to yourself, or can you open up your feelings to your friends? Talk to Jesus about this!

DAY 20

Song of Songs 1:9 (NIV)
I liken you, my darling, to a mare among Pharaoh's chariot horses.

Now we hear from the Lover for the first time. The Beloved has given us our first glimpse of His character, but we now catch a glimpse of how He sees her. From a twenty-first century perspective, to be described as a mare is quite hard to receive as a compliment. When we describe someone as looking like a horse it is usually derogatory and terribly unflattering. But here it is affirming of her beauty, strength and possible child-bearing capacity. He uses the word 'darling'. "My darling" is a description of someone beloved, and by saying this He is laying ownership of the love-bond between them, laying his feelings on the line.

A mare is a female horse – one who has, or who will, bear foals. So the Beloved is young and fertile. She is harnessed; therefore she must be strong and trained, able to work with others. And what is she harnessed to? A cart? A wagon? Is she part of a desert train? Used for manual labour? No, she is harnessed to Pharaoh's chariot. Pharaoh: the most important man in the land, who would only have the best; his chariot carrying him or one of his generals into battle. This has to be a place of high esteem in the horse world! The Lover is giving a description to the Beloved which shows that in His eyes there is no-one more perfect and no way can He honour her more highly.

I wonder how often we receive the accolades of others as insults or condemnation instead. How we need to know the speaker so that we can differentiate between accolade and insult! Often when we commend another we use words that are pleasing to us, things that bring us delight – but because we have different preferences another might receive our words quite differently.

Let me give you an example. Once our house group were reflecting on Revelation's description of our prayers; they are described as rising like incense to God. I personally find that incense makes me feel extremely nauseous, so the thought of my prayers rising to God and causing that effect on Him is not at all encouraging! In fact it could put me off praying for ever! Others, though, really enjoy the smell of incense and would probably like praying more if they knew their prayers would have such a pleasing effect on God.

The Lover, as well as describing the Beloved, is also revealing who He is. He's obviously been close to Pharaoh's chariots; otherwise he would not know what the horses were like. He is revealing how important a horse would be to Him... and therefore how important the beloved is to Him.

Although modern women would despise the thought of being harnessed and therefore controlled, there is a challenge here, because to be harnessed means "to be inextricably linked" and "to be controlled by"! The way that the harness is fitted will determine how the mare is controlled – or even if within a pair she is the one controlling. Which is better: to be harnessed to the King's chariot and be swift to answer to His controlling authority; or to be harnessed and chained to the tyrants of sin, shame, fear and anguish that nudge us imperceptibly in directions that we do not really wish to go?

Prayer & Contemplation: *To what are you harnessed? Invite Jesus to be Lord of every area of your life.*

DAY 21

Song of Songs 1:10-11 (NLT)
How lovely are your cheeks; your earrings set them afire! How lovely is your neck, enhanced by a string of jewels. We will make for you earrings of gold and beads of silver.

Is the Beloved wearing these things, or is the Lover imagining what she will be like when she is wearing them? What size the earrings must be if they reach down to her cheeks! None of your tiny little ear-rings just on the lobes for the Beloved! Great big ear-rings that frame her face are the order of the day. Not just a string of jewels for her neck but several! There is a real lavishness to this description of the Beloved. Why her cheeks and her neck? Maybe because those are the places she would wear jewels but maybe because those are the places the Lover would kiss her, and so he may already have had a fairly close inspection of her finery, her cheeks and her neck! Are her cheeks beautiful because of the ear-rings, or do the ear-rings enhance the beauty? The same goes for the neck!

The implication of verse 11 is that the Beloved's ear-rings, if she has any, are not made of gold and silver. The Lover is sharing His love by upgrading her jewellery. His love will make her even more beautiful than she already is. A gift of lavish generosity! Gold and silver would be signs of royalty, perhaps? Certainly of wealth! This portion all reads breathlessly, as if nothing is too much for the Lover in showing the depths of His love for the Beloved.

How will the Beloved feel on hearing the Lover's words and on receiving such lavish gifts? Will she rebuff the words and refuse the gifts? Pure surmising from experience suggests to me that she'll be overwhelmed with delight. Her self-worth which, let's face it, has been rock bottom, will rocket as she sees herself as the Lover sees her. The abundance He gives her will be held in her mind and her hands and will slowly percolate to her heart and soul! I wonder what will happen then when the lavishness of love meets the blackness of her sin. Will she still be able to receive the Lover's gifts?

Personal experience and sharing the experience of others leads me to conclude that it is highly likely that she will find all that's said and given difficult to receive in heart and soul and she may well not allow such generosity to touch the shameful depths of her being. How often do we hear in our own minds, or coming out of our own mouths, "I really don't deserve..." That's true on one level: we don't at all deserve! But grace looks beyond that level to the 'us' that God intended before creation and sees that He loves us despite our unreservedness; He still longs to give. Why? Why so lavishly? God's nature is lavish and extravagant. He cannot help Himself. 'Living in grace' means to, in ever greater measure, understand and appropriate this generous gift.

How would the Lover feel if the Beloved refuted all His words and refused all His gifts? Devastated! Wounded deeply! Rejected! How does God feel when we refuse the lavishness of His love? Much the same but in far greater measure! We struggle so much with grasping that Almighty God is in deep and bitter pain each time we choose to go our own way and follow our own beliefs about ourselves. We are such a rebellious people; we do not deserve anything from God! We struggle to receive His salvation after resisting for years because we refuse to humble ourselves. Then even having found Him faithful in saving us, we still refuse to humble ourselves further; the sorrow in the Father's heart over our choosiness has greater pain than that of a lover spurned.

Prayer & Contemplation: *Imagine these words to be spoken by Jesus to you. How does it make you feel? Can you receive his lavish love? If not, what holds you back? Talk to your Lover about it today!*

DAY 22

Song of Songs 1:12-14 (NLT)
The king is lying on his couch, enchanted by the fragrance of my perfume. My lover is like a sachet of myrrh lying between my breasts. He is like a bouquet of sweet henna blossoms from the vineyards of En-gedi.

This is the Beloved's response to the first utterances of her Lover. As He has chosen to liken her to things He finds appealing, so the Beloved returns with words describing Him in relationship to her. We've already pondered the fragrance and its effects. The Beloved is close enough for her perfume to spread its fragrance at the King's table. Is she a serving girl or is she an honoured guest? Is it really happening or is it deep in her earnest longings? Either way her presence is noticed and received as fragrant – a worthy gift.

Whether or not the Lover has actually rested between the Beloved's breasts we are left to surmise. The description leaves one reeling in the depths of the Beloved's longings. It stirs up deep longings in me for Jesus to be that close – permanently!

In those days a sachet would have been handcrafted, soft to the touch, sewn with love. Would the myrrh have been picked from her own garden?

Myrrh always brings thoughts of Christmas carols and the story of the Wise Men's visit to the infant Jesus. My mind leaps to the record of the death of Jesus and the distinct probability that myrrh was one of the embalming spices brought for His body. Myrrh always brings thoughts of sorrow and joy intertwined! How often I long for one and shun the other, but if I refuse the sorrow then I miss the joy too!

Prayer & Contemplation: *Do you desire to experience more of this intimacy with Jesus? His desire is even greater. Seek His presence today, and rest with Him for a while.*

DAY 23

Song of Songs 1:12-14 (NLT)
The king is lying on his couch, enchanted by the fragrance of my perfume. My lover is like a sachet of myrrh lying between my breasts. He is like a bouquet of sweet henna blossoms from the vineyards of En-gedi.

The aroma of myrrh resting between her breasts would always be wafting into the Beloved's sense. The deep longing to be intimate is consuming her. The warmth of her body would guarantee that the aroma of the Lover would always be filling her senses, always close to her heart.

Physical closeness is a deep human longing, one that I have often tried desperately to deny. Therefore I've lived permanently in the grief of not receiving such a gift and have made it impossible and painful for others to give it to me. The problem is exacerbated by being fearful that if I attempt physical closeness I will injure the focus of my attention by my clumsiness and inexperience or that my advances will be rejected, which I would receive as a rejection of who I am! And so the longing eats at me!

Why do I deny my longings? Is it that I do not want to have them – so if I pretend they're not there then I can ignore them? Have I been so hurt when sharing them in the past that it's safer to deny them? Do I really believe I can live without them? I certainly can 'merely exist' – I've done it for years – but that's left me empty. It's meant that life has been meaningless. I think, "Can I honestly allow myself to long for God that much? What if He doesn't come through for me, or I'm not 'good enough'?" I wonder if the Beloved had these doubts and fears. The fact that she'd been mistreated would suggest that she could readily identify with these thoughts.

Prayer & Contemplation: *Do you have to swim against a current of lies and doubts when you read these descriptive passages? Can you accept that He really means you? How do you respond when other people compliment you? Pray that the 'lie-listening' will be overtaken by 'truth-believing'!*

DAY 24

Song of Songs 1:13 (NLT)
My lover is like a sachet of myrrh lying between my breasts.

This is the Beloved describing graphically her Lover and how He attracts and brings life to three of her senses: smell, sight and sound.

The modern understanding of the word 'sachet' would be a packet containing a small amount (but just the right amount) of something. The contents are all important – the sachet is to be discarded; its sole purpose is to be a container. Similarly, our *soul* purpose is to be a container, a container of Jesus to be given liberally away and for others to come and take.

When this was written the sachet was probably not as unimportant as now. The sachet may have been hand-woven, certainly hand-sewn, to carry something precious like myrrh. It was probably quite ornate too. It would not have been disposable but prized and protected, to be refilled when the myrrh had been used or lost its potency!

I wonder what just the right amount of myrrh is... The words of the carol 'We Three Kings' come to mind:

Myrrh is mine. Its bitter perfume,
Brings a taste of gathering gloom,
Sorrowing, sighing, bleeding, dying,
Sealed in a stone cold tomb.

Yes, myrrh was used for embalming and preserving dead bodies. But I understand that the Beloved's desire was to use it as a preservative of her love for the Lover and the Lover's for her.

Then there's the fragrance! Resting between her breasts, warmed by her body heat, the fragrance would rise immediately to her nostrils – the scent of pleasure entering her body through her nose but soon infiltrating her whole being! Had the Lover actually lain between her breasts? Maybe! In which case this is a revealing of longing to experience again! Maybe He hadn't lain there, but such is her intense desire for Him to do so that this is her attempt to express her longing and delight as she waits for the time of its fulfilment. Will she be disappointed? Cynical life experience says that disappointment is inevitable. Spirit-filled hope says that consummation, complete fulfilment will come.

For the Lover to rest between the Beloved's breasts there will be a surrender on his part – an acknowledgment and 'living out' of his desire to be a child again, free from responsibilities and fully nurtured in the arms of one who loves intimately.

Prayer & Contemplation: *What is your heart's expectation when you come to God? Disappointment or fulfilment? Read Matthew 7:8-11, and ask the Father to increase your faith in His goodness.*

DAY 25

Song of Songs 1:14 (NLT)
He is like a bouquet of sweet henna blossoms from the vineyards of En-gedi.

En Gedi is described in the Thompson Chain-Reference Bible:

En Gedi – "means the fountain of the kid" is a celebrated place some 400 feet above the west shore of the Dead Sea, where immense fountains of warm water flow out from beneath limestone cliffs and cascades on down to a small but fertile plain half a mile broad and a mile long. Here, in ancient times, grew vineyards, palms, balsam, camphor, gum arabic, sugar cane, melons, and many other edible fruits and plants that made it one of the world's famed garden spots … Above and around the fountains are towering cliffs and a wild area called the wilderness of En Gedi, which no-one can overrate as a place of refuge. There are numerous caves in the area, some of which sheltered David and his followers when they dwelt here for some time in the "strongholds of En Gedi" 1 Sam 23:29. King Saul, with 3000 men, sought David on these "Crags of the Wild Goats" It was in one of these caves that David, unnoticed, cut off a corner of Saul's robe (1 Sam 24:22)[5]

Prayer & Contemplation:

"Your presence within, O Lover of my soul, makes me like En Gedi. You bring the fragrance and fruitfulness of En Gedi to my soul. You satiate me and bring me abundance for others to share.

"Lord I think I know the wilderness of En Gedi – only I've sometimes felt more like Saul searching for David rather than David being sheltered. I recognise I need to see this wilderness time as a friend not an enemy – a time to be relished and not resisted; a time to submit and not to struggle. These times are not boring, barren times to be endured; they are opportunities for spirit and soul-strengthening to be enjoyed – times of shelter and security, not lifeless tedium nor fearful emptiness. They are to heighten my longings and give me the choice to search after You with all my heart, mind, soul, spirit and strength. Despite the wilderness, fruitfulness and feasting are not far away."

---

[5] Quote taken from the Thompson Chain-Reference Bible (p.1659) with the permission of Kirkbride Bible Company

DAY 26

Song of Songs 1:14 (NLT)
He is like a bouquet of sweet henna blossoms from the vineyards of En-gedi.

In the Bible, the land around En Gedi is also referred to as the Wild Goat Rocks. Located on the western shores of the Dead Sea, these spring-fed waters (falls) provide pleasure for travellers today much as they did in ancient times.

Even the wilderness isn't a hostile place. In fact it is a place of solitude where I can meet alone with God, whereas the garden and springs of En Gedi are populous and popular. It is there that I will more likely be plundered – less opportunity to spend lengthy times alone with Him. We must welcome the wilderness as much as the fruitful garden.

The garden has boundaries and changes of scene. There is certainty and security, a pattern which is friendly in its predictability. The wilderness, however, seems to have no signposts, no boundaries, no landmarks, no end. It feels like an all-consuming vastness that never ends. Nothing to give any clues that God has even passed through, let alone taken up residence and is there to be found.

So often I demand a pleasant garden when Jesus desires to meet me in the wilderness – and as I find Him and meet Him, the wilderness blossoms into life because of His presence. Often I want to predict where He'll be and demand that I lie with Him on succulent grass rather than barren rock. So often '*where* I am' becomes more important than '*who* I am with'... and yet there He is, eagerly desiring to meet me! Sadly, I often look past His eagerness to my demands, and I push Him away.

The vineyards are probably the border between the lush lands of En Gedi and the vast wilderness of En Gedi – possibly on the slopes. How easy it is to long to pass through the vineyards, to be in the abundance, when all we seem to face is the bleakness of the wilderness. Even in the abundance of answered desire we are left bereft – alone again and hungry again!

Used symbolically the vine was the emblem of prosperity and peace amongst the ancient Hebrews – more specifically, the chosen people. They were the wine which God had taken out of Egypt (Psalm 53:8-14; Isaiah 5:1-5). They had been given all necessary attention for the production of outstanding fruit. But...

> *Henna ... "camphire" ... is a shrub originating in India. The pulverised leaves were made into a paste and used from earliest times as a cosmetic. Egyptian women employed it to dye their hair, finger and toe nails, hands and feet. Men coloured their beards with henna, and often the tails and manes of their horses. ... Any women thus adorned who fell captive to the Hebrews were required to remove all traces of the dye ... The orange or bright yellow colour probably had pagan associations. The shrub grows wild in Palestine, and may attain a height of twelve feet. It has spiny branches bearing clusters of whitish fragrant flowers at the tips.[6]*

This obviously would not refer to branches, only blossom. For the Beloved the overwhelming presence of the Lover is focused in His fragrance, a compliment to her fragrance at his table (v.12). The henna flowers do not appear startling, but their perfume must be the important feature. What must the aroma have been like – the Beloved's fragrance plus the myrrh plus the henna blossoms? An intoxicating cocktail which obviously was arousing!

Prayer & Contemplation: *Has 'where you are' become more important to you today that 'who you are with'? Thank Jesus today that He walks with you through the wilderness as well as through the vineyards. Enjoy your relationship with Him right where you are today.*

---

[6] Quote taken from the New Bible Dictionary (p.1311); published by Intervarsity Press

DAY 27

Song of Songs 1:15 (NASB)
How beautiful you are, my darling, how beautiful you are! Your eyes are like doves.

This is like a song, a refrain or a response. The next verse shows the Beloved echoing the same sentiments but to the Lover, and then the Lover comes back in again. In my mind I can almost hear the chorus accompanying these words: "Music is love looking for a word."

Eyes like doves!

- A pair of doves: the symbol of love. Doves mate for life, and when one dies the other quite literally dies of a broken heart.
- Doves: the symbol of purity. This is a statement of her virginity, a gift she is offering her Lover.
- Doves: the symbol of peace. There is a welcome invitation: come, visit my soul. The Lover has received the invitation and in response must have given His eyes – His doves – of welcome.

The beauty that the Lover sees, if He's looking through her eyes, is not the Beloved's outward beauty, however stunning that may be. Rather he is searching deep into her soul and seeing the perfected beauty of deep inner soul: the 'her' that is real and true and unspoiled. I sense this not being a bold and strident declaration of her beauty but an awed and whispered acclamation of wonder.

Prayer & Contemplation:

"How seldom we offer our eyes to You, Lord! So often we are shamed by our experience and our sinful choices. Just as the Beloved is ashamed by the darkness of her own skin, so we are shamed by the darkness of our selfish attitudes, and we lower our eyes so that You are not permitted entry to our souls. Forgive me! I offer my eyes to you once again today."

DAY 28

Song of Songs 1:16-17

She How handsome you are, my beloved! Oh, how charming! And our bed is verdant. _He_ The beams of our house are cedars; our rafters are firs.

The Beloved responds and looks into the Lover's eyes. His charm is not just outward but inner also.

Their bed is verdant – green, luscious, lavish, luxurious and a place of supreme comfort and security. To lie close to someone is to be close enough to see deeply into their soul should they so permit. Seeing deeply into another's soul must also mean that they can see into yours should they so desire. Such vulnerability! Such nearness! No closer place can be found on this earth – physically touching, eye-to-eye, an open invitation for all of one soul to entwine with all of another. No wonder, later on, the Beloved counsels not to awaken love until it so desires!

The word 'verdant' encourages me to think of a verse from the hymn "The king of love my shepherd is"[7]:

Where streams of living water flow
My ransomed soul He leadeth
And, where the verdant pastures grow,
With food celestial feedeth.

This hymn is based in Psalm 23 – a Psalm of David, who was Solomon's father! Did David sing his songs to Solomon; would he have taken Solomon to the streams and verdant pastures? I would like to think so. As Solomon was such a wise man (even before God gave him the gift of wisdom) and had a heart after God, I believe he must have experienced these things to have written so poetically about them. Hopefully David would have seen his experiences as a shepherd boy as foundational to his later role of 'good king' and would have offered Solomon those same foundations.

The words, both from Song of Songs and from The King of Love describe in my mind the lush valleys of En Gedi (referred to earlier). The bed is verdant: they lie in the pastures gazing contentedly and

---

[7] Henry W Baker (1821-1877)

intermittently at each other and at their surroundings, an idyllic surrounding made all the more spectacular by the love and passion between the pair of them.

Do you have a shared memory of being refreshed by the stillness of your surroundings, this made spiritually profound by the gift of another's soul? Somehow such amazing gifts become a love feast that so fill our emotional tanks that we believe we could go on forever and achieve anything asked of us – but how soon we use up the spiritual energy or succumb to the voice of fear.

The spreading branches of the wide cedar trees provide the canopy of shade for them; the tall, straight trunks of the fir trees provide the strength to protect them and their love. In this, with all the aroma of perfume, henna and myrrh, come the scents of grass, cedar and fir. So many fragrances – no wonder they are heady! I can just imagine them turning to each other and wishing that this could be forever... all those young lovers' hopes and dreams which with the cynicism of experience disintegrate into the humdrum tedium of responsibility and everyday life. Can these dreams hold and be fulfilled? From an earthly perspective and standpoint maybe not, but from a heavenly one there is hope in the promise of Jesus that paradise awaits.

Prayer & Contemplation: *The precious moments spent lovingly with another may be fleeting, but Jesus is forever ready in that place to be with you. Set aside time today to just be close to Him and enjoy His love and presence.*

DAY 29

Song of Songs 2:1 (NASB)
I am the rose of Sharon, the lily of the valleys.

Imagine with me a walk in the rose garden. The fragrance of the blooms, subtle in places and powerful in others, attracts like bees to the nectar as we feast our eyes on the beauty and splendour of the most well-known and well-loved of flowers.

If we chose to walk the rose gardens of the Holy Land then we'd head for Sharon, for in this luscious of places the best roses are to be found. The perfume of such a preponderance of flowers is heady. The sense of well-being in a rose garden brings resurrection life. See, mingled in, the lilies of the valley. Under spreading rose bushes they are hard to see, yet their daintiness beckons as their perfume pervades the air.

In our English climate they manage to grow in the most inhospitable of places, even forcing their way up through impossible terrain, to shout their presence above the clamour of harshness. For the Hebrew a lily would signify purity. In whiteness we would recognise the call to purity.

Prayer & Contemplation:

"Lord, every word in chapters two and three of Song of Solomon shouts 'closeness' to me. They announce that these deep longings are real and not to be denied. They draw me after You, and with the Beloved I long to run on doe's legs after You. The thought of the thrill of the chase brings a breathless feeling and deep internal anticipation – physical sensation, so physical it hurts. Just as if I'd run round the park, I gulp deep breaths of air to replenish oxygen, but as I've not been physically exerted the breaths sound more like deep, deep sighs. It seems like every nerve-ending on my skin is aroused and super-sensitive. I ache to be touched by Love's tenderness. No demands, no requests, no expectations, no hidden agendas, <u>no fear</u> – just love, just to be, just to be close, just to rest and be me and for it to be alright just to be me!"

DAY 30

Song of Songs 2:1 (NASB)
I am the rose of Sharon, the lily of the valleys.

It is a lily found in a valley – a valley, a place often of darkness and doubt but also the place of humility. If it is the Lover who speaks then what better description of Jesus, calling Himself a rose and a lily of the valley – beautiful, fragrant, pure and holy. If it is the Beloved who speaks, what a privilege to be able to recognise herself as having all those qualities. Only in a place of humility can we ever hope to grow purity. Jesus is made more pure by His obedience in the place of humility. It doesn't matter whether this is the Lover or the Beloved who speaks because it's true of both; the Lover dwells with and within the Beloved.

Prayer & Contemplation:

"As a statement of who I am in You, Lord, this draws worship from my soul. I feel adoration rising, but I also feel it descending; to see me filled with Your awesome purity is a glorious revelation which seems so understated in this statement, until I read behind the words and understand the significance of the choice of flowers and places.

"So often these things fall by the wayside as I assume you've picked a place or a thing out of thin air, but You are the Word and You choose and use words to their fullest meaning. For me to see myself as beautiful, fragrant, pure and humble seems impossible. Comparing myself with You, I see nothing but the dirt, filth and grime of my life. I look into the cesspool and see despair. But I look into your eyes and see my reflection, and there I know that I am those beautiful flowers. The warmth of Your tender touch convinces me that there is truth that lies behind my despair. I am being transformed into Your image and each small step along the way brings me closer to being a full image bearer."

DAY 31

Song of Songs 2:2-3 (NIV)
*He Like a lily among thorns is my darling among the young women.
She Like an apple tree among the trees of the forest is my beloved
among the young men. I delight to sit in his shade, and his fruit is
sweet to my taste.*

"I only have eyes for you..."Amongst all the other maidens, who
were no doubt beautiful too, the Lover only sees the Beloved. He
doesn't ignore the others, but by comparison they are just thorns! In
nature thorns and lilies don't grow together – at least not in western
horticulture. All the varieties are smooth and sleek, from water-lilies,
via lily-of-the-valley, to tiger lilies and death lilies; the entire spectrum
is smooth and thorn free! Would thorns grow near lilies in the Middle
East? Or is it referring back to the thorns on the rose bushes in verse
1? If so, it becomes even more amazing that the Lover is noticing the
lily and not the rose, where, in the natural, one would have thought
the rose to have been the more noticeable of the two!

I don't believe the Lover is being derogatory about the other
maidens but being emphatic about His desire for the Beloved. Such is
Jesus' commitment to the outcast and the oppressed, the small and
insignificant people of this world, that this verse should be impressed
on all our hearts – both from the perspective of how we might view
those considered 'not worth it' by society and that of how Jesus sees
us. We've already noted that the Beloved considers herself a poor
specimen and compares herself unfavourably. The Lover is doing all
He can to lift her self-worth and enable her to see that in His eyes the
other maidens wouldn't hold a candle to her!

An apple tree in a forest! A lily among thorns! These comparisons
show how both the Lover and the Beloved view each other as poles
apart from even the best of the rest. The items compared don't
naturally belong together. Just as lilies are not seen among thorns in
our habitat, how often do we see apple trees in forests? An apple tree
would be dwarfed and starved of light if it grew in a British forest!
The fruitfulness of the forest is for the creatures that dwell there.
Apple trees belong in orchards or gardens, and their fruit, whilst
feeding insects and birds, is predominantly for human consumption.

For apple trees to bear fruit they cannot be tightly packed or the light would not penetrate to ripen the fruit. The Beloved sees the Lover's fruitfulness. His fruit is sweet to her taste. Does this refer to the kisses of His lips? Yes! More than that? Possibly!

The Lover is the apple tree among the trees of the forest, the other young men! He is fruitful to her; they are not. They may be taller and stronger, but the Beloved has eyes only for her Lover. She delights to sit in His shade. It is her great longing to be there all of the time. She has fond memories of previous sojourns under his branches. Sheltered here, she is protected from the heat of the sun which has brought her her shame. In the dappled light her dark skin would not be so evident, but the brightness of her eyes and the aliveness of her smile would bring life to the Lover, and His responses would bring life to her soul. In the shade of the tree she has enjoyed and tasted his full fruitfulness; her shame has not prevented her enjoyment. Here she begins to believe that she is who He says she is; her shame and past experience begin to lose their power to chain her. She is free to be herself and to enjoy the relationship with her Lover to its fullest!

Prayer & Contemplation:

"Lord, I sit in my quiet space with you watching a candle burn. Oh, how I long to sit in the shade of Your apple tree and to feast on the sweetness of Your fruit! The world presses in, and its clamours make demands on me. As the aroma of the candle lingers, use it as a trigger to keep drawing me back to the shade of Your love. When Your whispers of love touch my soul I begin to believe that I am as beautiful as a lily among thorns, and when I believe that in my mind and feel it deep in my emotion then I begin to live as Your child. Even in my weakness I perceive that You love me and flow through me and that I can be the fragrant and beautiful lily You purposed for me to be, that the beauty and fragrance of my life will make a difference to You! Wow, what an honour! And it will make a difference to others.

"I am watered in my soul and my flower stands upright. I display all that I am, giving in beauty, giving myself away. Oh, that healing would come swiftly to all those who see themselves as thorns and not lilies – that the fulfilment of Paul's prayer for the Ephesians (1:18) would swiftly come about – so that we may all view You, ourselves and our relationships with spiritual eyes! What riches there are in seeing ourselves – lilies among thorns – as You see us!"

DAY 32

Song of Songs 2:4-6 (NIV)
Let him lead me to the banquet hall, and let his banner over me be love. Strengthen me with raisins, refresh me with apples, for I am faint with love. His left arm is under my head, and his right arm embraces me.

To refer to these verses as sexual may be frowned on by some interpreters of the Bible. But I cannot fathom why God should create us with erogenous zones if they were not meant to be part of our makeup – spiritual as well as physical, mental and emotional. God declares that we are fully known. He also declares that we are made in His image. Therefore it seems perfectly reasonable to me that God will have parts of His being that are there for no other reason than to bring Him pleasure. Mankind was created for this purpose, and we fell far short of God's desire for us and for Himself. When God said of Jesus, "This is my beloved Son; in Him I am well pleased,"[8] I don't see why that could not have been a totally profound pleasure in who He is, apart from what He would do. Not just an act that gave a squeal of delight. Not just a deed that brought forth actions of pleasure. I can imagine God's eyes opening wide and Him clasping His hands together with the tingle of a child opening a longed for present. Not just a thought that when worked through to its conclusion had a perfect result. No, this was total pleasure that caught all of that and more because it brought in God's emotions! No wonder the heavens and the earth trembled. All of God was and is totally delighted with Jesus, and because of Jesus God is totally delighted with you and me. No small wonder the angels have a party; God's delight is contagious!

Prayer & Contemplation: *Can you accept that God truly delights in you? That He deeply desires you? Ask Him to increase your understanding and experience of His love. Ask Him to heal anything that stands in the way.*

---

[8] Matthew 3:17

DAY 33

Song of Songs 2:5b (NIV)
...for I am faint with love.

I know what it is to be faint with hunger. Since my diabetes diagnosis it has become an acute signal – a signal that needs a rapid response. If I do not respond to my hunger pangs then I know I could be in for trouble. So shouldn't the same apply to the love pangs we all feel? It requires humility to own a need for love, and yet it is a necessity for us all if we are to live. Without love we merely exist. With the incorrect type of love we *think* we live – but it's fleeting, here and gone, never fully satisfying, leaving us craving for more that in turn drives us to making unwholesome choices. When Jesus comes and touches us with His love, our entire being responds – body, mind, emotion, soul and spirit. We can become faint with love; we have to be carried and tended and caressed and cherished and nurtured. In a physical faint we can do nothing for ourselves except fall over. In a spiritual faint we should do nothing for ourselves but humbly submit and allow the Holy Spirit to carry us to the Lover of our souls. There's the rub! Our human pride so often baulks and will not allow us to own our weakness, and so we arrogantly miss out on the best Jesus has to offer. We choose to become like the dogs and eat the crumbs from the table when we could be feasting at the banquet.

When we choose to feast we understand in minute portions what it means to be faint with love. Is that a paradox? Maybe! But then so much of faith's experience is a paradox because it defies any human logic and reason! Who else would die to demonstrate complete love? When we are faint with Love, the command not to awaken love until it so desires becomes more understandable because the passion is completely insatiable! My humanity would demand that this love be satisfied *now* and the cravings of the flesh would expect fulfilment and satisfaction. The disappointment of not finding that fulfilment risks finding its expression in all sorts of demanding and potentially debased and sinful choices!

The cry is for strength and refreshing because I am faint with love. Love weakens me, it overcomes me, it overrules me; I cease to merely exist as I begin to... live. To be poured into by love is more physically debilitating than to be poured out in love. To stay in the middle, satiated, is to be fit to burst.

"Look!" "Listen!" "Feel!" Are these childish responses? I think not! Childlike? Certainly! I can be nothing else before a God who lives and loves in ways beyond my earthly experience. I am a novice, a beginner, a 'rookie', an upstart when it comes to either giving or receiving love. It is quite ridiculous that I should attempt to display it, let alone describe it! To practice the presence of God is to choose to be in a state where He may choose to reveal His love. I can ask Him to display it in a certain way and in a certain place, but in the asking I risk being so focused on my demands that I completely miss the revelation He is giving.

Prayer & Contemplation:

"God, Your image can be found in everyone and in everything. Each person is more than they claim or that I perceive them to be. Even if I give them as much of myself as I know how to give – even if they gave me as much as they know how to give and as much of You as they know how to give – we will still fall far short of relating in godly unity. There is a sense, humanly speaking, in which this has 'failure' written right across it, and if I look at that label I give up, I do not take the risk; the dare is rejected, and we are all the poorer for that choice. Spiritually there is another label; it says, 'Adventure and hope, this way!' It's fraught with human and relational danger, but if I listen above the clamour of risk I hear, "I love you, child," and the yearning in my soul to be wooed to as total a satisfaction as is currently possible draws me on.

"'I love' calls forth faith, and I am asked to believe that all things are possible! Do I crave signs, wonders and miracles? Can I believe they will happen? Where is my grain of mustard seed? If I hold and offer it in the palm of my open hand, will it be ignored? Will it be seen? Will it be blown away by the merest puff of wind? Will I ask in faith believing that I have already received? I am challenged by how small my faith is to believe for Your 'more'. How do I hold contentment and satisfaction in my soul along with the yearning, longing, for fulfilment that will only be in glory?"

DAY 34

Song of Songs 2:4 (RSV)
He brought me to the banqueting house, and his banner over me was love.

He *brought* me. This is written in the past tense; therefore I am there! It is not a future event with all its 'might's or 'if's or 'maybe's.

The banquet hall speaks of a huge, vast table, fully laden. Is the hall full of people? If it is, are they intrusive? Or are we alone? Where are we sitting? Close? At opposite ends of the table? Where are His eyes fixed? And mine?

What is a love feast/banquet? Is it choice food? Or is it character, personality or virtues? Is the feast just for my mouth to taste? Or is it for all my senses? (Is it for others too?) Is it a feast for my soul? How will I experience that? Are there words to describe this soul-feast? "Music is love in search of a word."[9] Are there musical notes to record the soul's song?

As a human…

- I can give physical food – to eat and drink
- I can give physical food – to smell and taste
- I can give emotional food – to touch and sense
- I can give sexual food – to feel and enliven
- I can give sensual food – to enrich and experience

I can give… but I have to be received. For me to receive, others have to give… and I have to be receptive. How do I become receptive? By experience, by faith, by trust, by being open, by being available, by being surprised, by taking risks.

His banner over me is love; that means *all* of Him in every aspect of His humanity and His divinity.

Prayer & Contemplation: *God, who is love, knows how to love you perfectly and completely. Share your feelings with Him. Imagine the banqueting table he has prepared for you, and thank Him.*

---

[9] Sidney Lanier

DAY 35

Song of Songs 2:6-7 (NIV)
His left arm is under my head, and his right arm embraces me.
Daughters of Jerusalem, I charge you by the gazelles and by the does
of the field: do not arouse or awaken love until it so desires.

Coldly and clinically, these two verses speak of actions performed by the Lover to the Beloved. They are an expression of His delight at being with her, a promise of what is to be once they are married. As she has the imminent hope of marriage, I expect that she is more readily able to rein in her desires to wait until she is legally secure in the relationship. From her place of security she can offer wise advice because she can see that such closeness brings so much passion to the surface that it would be all too easy to overstep the mark.

To bring emotions to the surface immediately makes the task of remaining 'within the rules of decency' immensely difficult. The Beloved, if we understand she comes from an abused background, will find this attention by her Lover overwhelming and confusing. Thus far the males she has been close to have used her and destroyed her self-worth. How easy it is when one man shows affection, consideration and affirmation to go overboard. Suddenly feelings of value, significance and love rise out of the dungeons we've placed them in and they swamp us to the point where reason and logic fly out of our minds and the need to be satisfied demands fulfilment. The passion to feel good about ourselves and to feel worth something to another just has to be right – and for those fleeting moments of ecstasy we receive what we think are our hearts' desires, only to find we've been duped; those heights that we rose to only serve to give us an even bigger drop into the pit of despair. The Beloved is so right to pronounce caution! Such are human relationships – even good, right, moral and legal ones – because they involve humans in their full humanity, let us down and destroy who we are.

Do not arouse or awaken love until it so desires! If love chooses when to be aroused or woken, there is a degree to which the emotion will dictate action. Making love an 'it' gives a sense that it is outside our (or anyone else's) control. Within our makeup we are created to be love, as God is love. But we must understand love in its fullness of expression and not limit it to sexual activity. There is the danger that, by leaving our faulty perception of love to be in control of our actions, we may leave ourselves open to regular assault and frequent failures. Love is as much 'who we are' as it is 'who God is' except that in this existence we wrestle with this part of who we are in the light of a human, sinful, selfish nature whereas God is love in the strength of His godly, perfect, self-giving nature. We must awake that part of God within us – for we fail in being His image-bearers if we don't – but we must also use our God-given logic and reason, based firmly on the foundation of His Word, to ascertain when our love nature is operating from holy or unholy passions.

Pure love is aroused by the Spirit; it will never contravene Scripture and it will always give for the holy good of another. When it gives only for what it might receive in return then it has to be doubted if it is pure love and not lust operating under the guise of grace!

Prayer & Contemplation: Are there areas in which your 'love' for another has left you open to assault, failure or sin? If so, ask God to heal your faulty perception of love and to free you to love by His Spirit. Ask Him to forgive you for the wrong you have done – and determine in your heart to forgive those who have wronged you. This may be a process, but you can begin it today.

DAY 36

Song of Songs 2:8-9 (NASB)
Listen! My beloved! Behold, he is coming, climbing on the mountains, leaping on the hills! My beloved is like a gazelle or a young stag. Behold, he is standing behind our wall, he is looking through the windows, he is peering through the lattice.

The Beloved is describing love being acted out from the place of being a responsive recipient. Anticipation is high – breathless just by watching love's exertions.

Very active and picture-provoking verbs are used: climbing, leaping, looking, peering. They are very specific, subjective and persistent.

Listen! Look! Childlike responses of wonder are offered – with an eagerness to share the delight with others. How essential it is to be drawn to the Lover's gaze! How often we baulk and feel unworthy! How often we are too busy to even notice his ardent searching and wooing! Have we ever begun to realise just how intense the Lover's search for our gaze is? Our search should be equally intense; instead we are drawn by the temptations and lures of this world and our own sinfulness.

Prayer & Contemplation: *Choose to slow down today, enough to become aware of the Lover's gaze. Become aware that Jesus is with you, loving you, in every situation you encounter.*

DAY 37

Song of Songs 2:10-13 (NASB)

My beloved responded and said to me, 'Arise, my darling, my beautiful one, and come along. For behold, the winter is past, the rain is over and gone. The flowers have already appeared in the land; the time has arrived for pruning the vines, and the voice of the turtledove has been heard in our land. The fig tree has ripened its figs, and the vines in blossom have given forth their fragrance. Arise, my darling, my beautiful one, and come along!'

Here the Beloved remembers of the Lover's words to her. She must have known the Lover's intense excitement. The words 'arise' and 'behold' are not commands; they are ejaculations of delight, a delight that has to be shared with one who would know and receive the joy and delight and be transformed by it.

There is a sense in which the barrenness of 'who the Beloved is' is being transformed to flower and fruit by the urgent love of the Lover. The touch of Jesus is bringing healing and restoration to a soul crippled by years of neglect – personal neglect and neglect by others.

How did the Beloved know the Lover was talking to *her?* Perhaps she was the only one there. Or perhaps she had heard Him call her by that precious intimate love-name, known only to him and her – a whisper on the breeze that pierced barriers – and she knew, every single part of her knew, that the words were for her alone. This is experiential knowing that makes every sensor vibrant and alive.

Prayer & Contemplation:

"Lord, the longing to hear Your voice speak to me is intense! I am confident that You actually want to do this for me – not because You have to, out of duty, but because You want to out of desire. I choose to believe that I am Your beautiful one. I can see – with my physical eyes but so much more with my spiritual eyes. I can see my soul reflected in Your eyes, and it's quite unbelievable!

"'Come with Me!' You say. The old me would say, 'Tell me where. Let me get things in control. Let me be prepared for any eventuality.' But the restored, new me says, 'Anywhere, Lord, just so long as it's with You!'"

DAY 38

Song of Songs 2:12b,14 (NIV)
...the cooing of doves is heard in our land ... My dove in the clefts of the rock, in the hiding places on the mountainside, show me your face, let me hear your voice; for your voice is sweet, and your face is lovely.

Today's text refers to *our* land. This could be the royal 'we'; the Lover is then speaking in speech reported by the Beloved. Or it could be the land wherein the Lover and Beloved are currently found, or in the land where they are headed, or in the 'land' that is their souls.

Having reported the Lover as saying the cooing of doves is heard in the land, the Lover then declares that His dove is in the clefts in the rock – in the hiding places on the mountainside. The cooing He hears is of doves plural, but *His* dove is hiding and He wants to hear her voice.

Prayer & Contemplation:

"Lord, is my voice in all its forms – the loud, proclaiming voice; the pained, shouting voice; the desperate voice; the chatty voice; the voice whispering sweet nothings; the singing voice singing victory songs and love songs; the voice of compassion; the voice of passion – on fire for You? Is it sweet to You?

"Lord, I become aware of all the modes my voice employs, and I realise that much as You love to hear my voice, there must be times when I am silent – totally focused on You with not even my conscious thoughts speaking about anything. If possible I would long for my subconscious thought to be silent too, totally fixed on You – with You filling all my vision."

DAY 39

Song of Songs 2:12b,14 (NIV)
...the cooing of doves is heard in our land ... My dove in the clefts of the rock, in the hiding places on the mountainside, show me your face, let me hear your voice; for your voice is sweet, and your face is lovely.

Are the hiding places referred to shared secrets – perhaps shared secret places? Or is the dove hiding so the Lover cannot find her? There is something endearing and wooing about our hiding places being a shared secret with Jesus. But if the places are hidden *from* Him then quite the reverse is true. Of course, He knows all things; He knows where the 'dove' is. But if it is the dove's choice to hide then she will not be found. Even if He is right by her side she will not receive Him and therefore will feel lost and alone, comforted only by the protection the rock affords.

Where is this mountainside? Could it be the mountain the Beloved has constructed to protect herself from all and sundry? Has she still not realized that she can never hide from the Lover, but only from herself? Is it the mountain of self? Faith the size of a mustard seed moves mountains! We see problems and people as mountains, but the mountain with the most potential for obscuring the view is our 'self' – the proud, arrogant, rebellious bit that screams, "I did it my way!"

The Lover has a heart longing to hear the love-song of the dove, to see the radiance of love on the face and in the eyes of the dove. But it is just that: a request not a demand. Pure love cannot demand; it can only ask and wait and hope.

Prayer & Contemplation:

"Lord, Your expectation and longing was, and is, that men would choose to love You and relate intimately with You. Your passion is the emotional response to Your disappointment! Wow, Lord! This is a sorrow that I cannot comprehend. Such an emotional response, that gives all of itself to see the longing fulfilled, overwhelms me. And it is amazing to ponder that your sorrow is deepened if I do not respond to your call. You do all this so that we might know something of how You feel about us!"

DAY 40

Song of Songs 2:15 (RSV)
Catch us the foxes, the little foxes, that spoil the vineyards, for our vineyards are in blossom.

At first glance this verse doesn't seem to fit; the temptation is to ignore it, to pass it over, pretend that it isn't there! Why does it come after a verse about doves? Is it that the dove's song would charm the foxes out of their lairs that they may then be snared? Foxes and doves don't naturally go together; the former would eat the latter. But there would be enticement. The margin text for this verse in the Thompson Chain Reference Bible (NIV) refers to 'little evils' – those things that we too would almost turn a blind eye to; those things which from a worldly standpoint are negligible in the 'evil' stakes. For example, 'little white lies' that we tell are considered more than okay; they are considered necessary!

They vineyards are in bloom – ready for fertilisation and to make flowers into fruit that are needed to sustain life. They are 'our' vineyards too; they belong to both the Lover and the Beloved. If the vineyard represents either the life of the Beloved or her life with the Lover – tainted by the world, self and sin – then is this command to consider those things which we consider 'necessary evils' to survive? If so, this is a call to purity!

Does this verse come because the Beloved needs to speak out, to confess even, those seemingly small things (for they mar the growth of the vineyard), the potential for fertility being corrupted by the 'little foxes'? The vineyard is ruined by the little foxes – not destroyed – for I guess, in the natural, foxes would not completely destroy a vineyard. Yet the damage they do would reduce its yield. The viticulturist would want maximum yield and would therefore do his utmost to keep the foxes out. The Lover desires the fullest expression of the fruit of their love relationship, but with the 'little sins' the potential for the crop is diminished.

Perhaps here the Beloved is satisfied with where she is and the love she is receiving, yet the Lover is exhorting her that there is still more. Is that why she's hiding in the rocks? Aware of her short-comings, shame has overcome her, and so she has beaten a track to the place of 'security' in the mountains, where she lives believing that her 'little foxes' will not matter, whereas the Lover is saying that they have to be caught. For their sakes, "Catch for us the little foxes." He is disappointed that he does not yet have the full love of the Beloved. He longs for her to be released. Vineyards in bloom are beautiful. The fragrance is alluring (verse 13) but the fragrance is not what the vineyards are intended for. It's only half their purpose. The fertilization of the blooms to produce the fruit is essential for a vine to be fulfilled, completed. To follow the sexual imagery, the Lover's desire is to infiltrate, to impregnate – he's drawn by the fragrance – but 'the little foxes' ruin the potential for fruitfulness; they get in the way of the consummation of the relationship.

If this season of blooming is not consummated, then this harvest is ruined – the potential for full intoxication lost! A full circle must be traversed to again reach the point of preparation for fullness. It is not a totally hopeless situation, but the potential for this season risks being lost. Each 'blossom season' brings potential; each yielding and chasing out of the foxes releases the vineyard to a fuller potential. Like succeeding years of falling in love with Jesus, the vineyard can either be more freed, more ready, more prepared or it can be more overgrown, more defeated, more ruined. The command is, "Catch!" The Beloved has to be active in the catching of the foxes, but I don't believe she works in isolation (that would be a task too great and be hopeless). The fact that she works in the presence of the Lover means that one step of willingness on her part, to deal with the foxes, releases Him to use His energy too to catch them.

Prayer & Contemplation: *What are the 'little foxes' that spoil your relationship with Jesus? Confess them to Him now and ask Him to deal with them.*

> *"Lord, I want to catch the little foxes so that our vineyard may fulfil its potential!"*

DAY 41

Song of Songs 2:16-17 (NIV)
My beloved is mine and I am his; he browses among the lilies. Until the day breaks and the shadows flee, turn, my beloved, and be like a gazelle or like a young stag on the rugged hills.

We can have a longing to possess those whom we love. There is a pure sense in which that is a holy desire, but flesh and sin have corrupted the desire. Instead of being a spiritual desire to possess God and be possessed by Him, our desire demands to be filled immediately by people and things. Then sin prevents us from possessing our inheritance now. The sadness that we endure can be constructive in driving us to Him or destructive in driving us, demanding, from others. There is an acceptance to be reached that chooses to wait and diverts energies into self-giving so that others may know the depths of their longing for Him.

In my own soul, I see the rebellion that has refused to belong, refused to give to anyone – least of all to Jesus! My demanding has resulting in *using* Him and others. But behind the rebellion, when self has been denied, I have felt the deep, deep longing to be totally consumed, to be so completely known that there is no need to hide or pretend.

Prayer & Contemplation:

"Lord, I know You fully know me. I've known it in my experience. The more I know You know, the more I struggle in the paradox of hiding and revealing... like the dove in the cleft of the rocks. She was hiding out of choice, but was she hiding out of fear or with squeals of delight? Probably the former – but what pleasure there is in hiding in order to spring a surprise! I know I can surprise my brothers and sisters – but can I really surprise You? When I choose to let You deeper into me, is it a surprise to You? Just as the time of Your coming again is in the Father's hands, is it possible that You are taken unawares by the beauty of my self-revelation? Do You feel this pain of love? Are You open-mouthed by the beauty of the revelation of grace in me?"

DAY 42

Song of Songs 2:16-17 (NIV)
My beloved is mine and I am his; he browses among the lilies. Until the day breaks and the shadows flee, turn, my beloved, and be like a gazelle or like a young stag on the rugged hills.

The physical longing for sexual union with my husband can become all-consuming, and the disappointment of it not happening profound, and the deep joy of entering into such a state profound beyond words. The disappointment and the joy both feel crushing and overwhelming.

Prayer & Contemplation:

"Lord, the spiritual longing for complete union with You feels like it kills me; I die, the longings fade and You fill my sight, or at least thoughts of You. How I long to stay here, and yet even here the cries of the mundane distract my attention.

"You browse among the lilies. We browse, consider each other deeply, enjoy the experience; we are heady with perfume and besotted by the beauty. You tenderly caress, and each flower's head turns and waits expectantly for their consummation. Not one is missed, not one over-looked. This is a deeply, longing scrutiny that melts even the hardest heart.

"Such is Your prowess, Lord, that rugged hills provide You with a delight rather that a challenge. Could it be that in my current frame of mind I am more like rugged hills than rolling ones?"

DAY 43

Song of Songs 3:1 (NIV)
All night long on my bed I looked for the one my heart loves; I looked for him but did not find him.

Such passion! Such yearning! Such pain! All night long!

A night is long! Lie awake with a howling child, a raging toothache, a mind-numbing fear or deep emptiness and the darkness becomes intensely black, the time drags interminably and the loneliness eats into the soul like no earthly definition can adequately describe. In the long night is nothing but despair. Your pit beckons and the slow slide into it becomes inevitable.

Despair: "Why can't I do anything to make it better?"

Reply: "Helpless!"

Despair: "Will it ever end?"

Reply: "Eternal!"

Despair: "Why now when love seemed so full, free and fragrant?"

Reply: "Empty!"

Why despair? *Why?* Because the joy of love experienced is so immense that when it is no longer available it feels as if life itself has been ripped away!

Joy and despair are flip-sides of the same coin. By 'fluke of chance' each flip of the coin brings hope for joy but almost equal probability of despair! No wonder the counsel is not to waken love until it so desires!

"All night long" is not only black but cold. The coldness of being alone wraps its icy tentacles around body, soul and spirit and squeezes rationality out! Logic brings no hope; it just seems to play mind games. It reasons there is no escape, and as we come to terms with the finality of our state, logic drips a droplet of hope, lighting the path again... But the fact is we're alone in our bed. We know that, it is our current experience; a hand reached out will confirm our aloneness! But such drips send us spiralling off on the merry-go-round again. Before we know it, love's beautiful tapestry wool has entangled itself into the unending mess of what-ifs, if-onlys and maybe's! Where one emotion, one thought, begins and ends is impossible to see in the snared jungle that is my soul.

A Walk in the Lover's Garden

Why love? Because when I know I am loved then I know and feel that I am alive. Because when I love and my love is received then I know and feel I am special and acceptable. Why love? Because I am made in God's image and He is love.

Prayer & Contemplation:

"Lord, do You look all night for the one Your heart loves? Oh, the pain in the father-heart of God each time You look for me and I'm not where You long for me to be – by Your side! Like the Beloved, You come looking. Like the Beloved, You do not find, for I choose so often to be elsewhere, unaware of Your great longing, choosing rather to be indulging myself in earthly titillations because I have no earthly manifestation of You. My choice causes You to grieve, and it may provide me with immediate thrill but it leaves me to grieve too, for my emptiness and loneliness are not filled by earthly loves. They are only consummated by Your presence – deep, intimate and real; emotionally, physically, mentally and spiritually satisfying."

DAY 44

Song of Songs 3:1 (NIV)
All night long on my bed I looked for the one my heart loves; I looked for him but did not find him.

Is this an ironic juxtaposition or divine coincidence? To wait helplessly while my flesh and blood suffers in anguish is not a place of my choice! To watch and listen whilst the Beloved pours out her feelings, trying desperately to label and acknowledge them... but it's all so new and seems so very unfair.

To hear in one breath that her 'Lover' feels as she does and then in the next breath to be told, "It will not work so it must never start," must be like being torn in two – wrenched apart in the soul. It seems like the biggest tease ever, a trick to destroy the soul. What can I do? What will my Lover do? What can I pray?

Prayer & Contemplation:

"Lord, what was 'right' in a king even looking at a dark-skinned vineyard worker? What hope had the Beloved for ever considering that the king might have pure and noble purposes towards her? In its allegory form, Song of Songs brings the hope of the King of Heaven choosing to form a deep and intimate relationship with even the most undeserving of His people. In human terms, Song of Songs is the stuff fairy tales are made of. You can even see the headlines: 'Servant girl made good'. In the cold light of reality, fairy tales do not stand up to scrutiny; they crumble as every part is bathed in logic's light. Is it a fairy tale that You, God, loved so much You died to have an 'unreal' and undeserved relationship with me? In the dark nights it is inconceivable; no-one could even think about stooping so low! But in the experience of my soul our relationship is a reality; no-one can take away those memories of tender touches, sweet caresses and loving whispers. What can't be, is!"

DAY 45

Song of Songs 3:1 (NIV)
All night long on my bed I looked for the one my heart loves; I looked for him but did not find him.

In the dark night of my soul I look for You, I long for You, and like the Beloved my senses tell me You're not there – a blanket slips over my soul-memory! My search becomes frantic and I forget to "Be still and know..."[10]

For every taste of joy, contentment and satisfaction it seems there is a mountain to struggle up and, after, a chasm to fall into. All the while the joy seems to dissipate before your eyes. Like grains of sand slipping through the fingers, it never lasts; even its memory seems to stir up the sludge and dilute it further. The chasm seems long and dark; the shafts of light, of intimate love, few and far between; the desperation to find the next all-pervasive touch strong; and reason flies out of the window.

We hear the desperation in the Beloved's voice: "All night long..." It is an interminable night when time stands still and hope lies buried, seemingly never to rise again. Grief is overwhelming. Surely the Lover must be here somewhere?

I deny the reality that my physical senses are telling me. I feel rejected, cast aside, left alone; anger and resentment eat my soul. I know I'll go look for Him. Help me find Him and I'll do anything for you. I'll bargain my very existence away for one more touch of His hand. I do not want to feel the pain of my sadness, so I crawl back to the beginning of grief's vicious circle and deny again what my senses tell me. Won't someone, anyone, stop this tread-wheel and let me off?

Prayer & Contemplation:

"Lord, nothing is more lonely than an empty bed when every part of body, soul and spirit longs to be loved. What must I do to make it better? Truth is, nothing will make it better until I accept that I am helpless to do anything. When I can be still, be really still, then I may know that You are God. The rebellion of my human soul cannot easily accept that answer, and I find that

---

[10] Psalm 46:10.

I can only be in that place fleetingly, but even then I risk seeing it as effort on my part that has gained its reward, rather than grace on Your part that loves in spite of my 'self'."

DAY 46

Song of Songs 3:1 (NIV)
All night long on my bed I looked for the one my heart loves; I looked for him but did not find him.

My inheritance is to be like Jesus. My inheritance is to be in the image of God. My inheritance is humility. My inheritance is to give. In the struggle to live in my inheritance, do I long often enough for the One my heart loves? How often is often? I guess that the ultimate often is always. Is that ever possible this side of glory? Or by the time I reach always have I breathed my last breath?

My measuring stick is Jesus, and in this life I will never attain His image. I am tempted to shrug my shoulders, resign myself to that fact, grit my teeth and get on with making myself to be as much like Jesus as I can be. Is there a point at which I can grieve my loss of 'self' and loss of 'image of God' and stop beating myself up? Can I move into acceptance that although those things are lost to me that God will make even better purposes than if I had remained whom He created me to be and if I had remained image-bearer without having fallen?

What is 'better' than being image-bearer? Answer: *restored* image-bearer! Restored image-bearer shows even more of Jesus' character. It brings hope to fallen mankind. If fallen man only ever saw perfection in Jesus they could not believe in being made perfect; it would be too lofty, too far, too impossible for them to even contemplate attempting. That is one of the reasons He was crucified. Man could not stand to see perfection – it presented too great a challenge – and so man attempted to prove he was better than perfection by destroying it. In my struggles to be 'restored image-bearer' I bring hope that would otherwise not have been possible. From my fallenness others see that the challenge is possible and that this inheritance can be theirs too.

This truth feels joyfully hopeless and hopelessly joyful! It brings the pain of those who won't try, the pain of those who as of yet can't try, and it brings the pain of those who are trying. Sometimes I wonder, why so much pain? But pain always prompts a response! Jesus longs that the response will always be one of turning to Him. The longing in His heart is for every soul to choose Him. Without pain there will be no chance of response, and no response means no opportunity for Him to reassign the inheritance. He desires us to walk this path. In Him eyes we are worthy of such honour. He can trust us with *His* pain. Others can trust us with theirs when we trust Him with ours. On earth, pain twists and contorts face, body and soul. In Heaven, pain brings forth more love, more grace, more mercy, more healing, more of God.

This seems logically perverse. Are there windows of hope in this pain? Windows that we can see the Cross through? Yes, *every* window is the Cross. Where the Cross is, there is always hope. Where the Cross is, there is faith in abundance. Where the Cross is, there is love unending. The Cross is in our heart, the Cross is in our soul, the Cross is in our spirit.

Prayer & Contemplation:

"Jesus, You invite me to pick up Your Cross daily. It seems too much! But I cling to Your promise that You will never leave me nor forsake me. I cling to Your promise that You will give me strength to endure. I will daily pick up Your Cross."

DAY 47

Song of Songs 3:2 (RSV)
I will rise now and go about the city, in the streets and in the squares; I will seek him whom my soul loves. I sought him, but found him not.

Those last few words echo like a song refrain, and with each repetition the disappointment and frustration is deeper and more painful.

If I went round an earthly city by night looking for my Lover I would only be able to find him if he so chose. In reading these verses I almost sense the Beloved is racing frantically in her night clothes round the streets – an erstwhile Wee Willie Winkie! Are these real streets? Is she actually physically out in the town? Or is she rehearsing in her tired but desperate mind all the places where she and the Lover have been and have enjoyed themselves and where she hopes he may be found?

This is not a casual looking, a passing of cursory glances! It's a 'rip the place apart' frantic searching as if the Beloved's very existence depends upon a positive result. To be so lonely is to die a lingering, frantic death without hope. Clutching at the vaguest of straws, we take succour from the tiniest morsel of hope. We hope in vain if our hope is in the things of this world. The kiss of a man in his fallen state can never compare with the honey from the lips of the Lover.

Prayer & Contemplation:

"Lord, I can identify with these words as my mind skips from place to place. My heart longs to find You, to feel You close; the whisper of Your breath in my soul seems too remote to hope for. Clinically my mind reasons that I only imagined that I met You; there is no 'five senses proof' that You've ever been there. If I listen to my mind, then with the Beloved I enter the stark reality of my empty bed and the empty streets – and my search is in vain. But when I tune out of the thoughts, reason, facts and logic that bombard my mind from the demands of the world, I enter into the secret chambers of my soul. There I see Your fingerprints. They have left an imprint that burns like a hot knife through butter. My mind and soul wrestle about which of them holds reality."

DAY 48

Song of Songs 3:3 (RSV)
The watchmen found me, as they went about in the city. "Have you seen him whom my soul loves?" Scarcely had I passed them, when I found him whom my soul loves. I held him, and would not let him go until I had brought him into my mother's house, and into the chamber of her that conceived me.

In a physical sense the watchmen were those who guarded the gates, manned the watchtowers, kept out intruders, warned of invaders – key people who kept the city safe. They'd watch for fires and may even have been a type of police, watching for thieves, etc. – quite powerful people! Maybe the Beloved would normally have had little or nothing to do with them.

They found *her,* and not the other way round. She was obviously behaving in a way that attracted attention. Did she know them? The question she asks of them may indicate that – after all, she gave no name or description. There is little for them to 'go on' in her words. Or is it this frantic despair that is causing her irrational behaviour and unreasonable statements? Either way the watchmen were of little help. You can sense her desperation rise with each step taken.

When I look inside me I wonder if there are 'watchmen' that I would ask for help, advice and information? With earthly watchmen there are some who are totally trustworthy and some who are definitely not (and it is almost impossible to tell them apart). So it is with spiritual watchmen. But we often seek out those who will give us the answer we want to hear. We even seek those watchmen who are not real people but who are the twisted voices of people who reside inside our heads. There are so many avenues to take to help us assess the correct choice and so many blind alleys leading to deeper darkness, despair and frustration. Was the Beloved wise to approach the watchmen? Am I wise to approach my watchmen? Wisdom lies in the choice of watchmen; they must shine the light of truth and speak with the love of Christ. How hard they are to find!

Prayer & Contemplation: *Can you identify the 'watchmen' in your life that you seek answers from? Do you use those watchmen because they tell you what you want to hear, or because they offer wisdom?*

DAY 49

Song of Songs 3:5 (NIV)
Daughters of Jerusalem, I charge you by the gazelles and by the does of the field: do not arouse or awaken love until it so desires.

My husband and I are learning such beautiful things about each other, how to initiate a response, how to yield when we may not fully feel like it; we are communicating when things give us pleasure rather than mechanically going through the motions. I guess we're finding our sensuality. Much of this, I know, is a release in me from all the wrong ways I've used my sensuality and my sexuality in the past. Pent up emotions are being released and the intensity of the passion is good. As long as I allow them to be controlled by God, I know they will always be used in the right way.

God is releasing my feelings, and I am to use them to bring pleasure and comfort to others. Passion is not to be shunned in any of its forms, but it is to be handled correctly. None of the feelings are wrong in themselves; it is what I do with them, the choices I make on how to display them, that could be wrong – the demands I make on another to meet them.

Without raised passions nothing gets done in the Kingdom because we all sit back and allow things to happen around us. If we use our passions to challenge us to move out then our motives will be godly. If we use our passions to demand that others meet our needs, our motives are self-seeking.

Prayer & Contemplation:

"Holy Spirit, I am so glad that it's You who has control of the passionate side of me. Were it not so, I would live in perpetual fear of getting it wrong and therefore not doing anything at all; whereas with You in control I know my passion will be fired in the correct way. Keep firing my passions but also keep controlling how I use them. Lord, I would go often to your chambers. If I feel the door has been shut, I know it's not You that's keeping it shut but me. As Your light consumes all the darkness, I see the path to the door and I race along it, my heart pounding within, because I know that whilst the bliss of marital union is a passion consumed, the bliss of spiritual union is ecstatic."

DAY 50

Song of Songs 3:5b (NIV)
Do not arouse or awaken love until it so desires.

My Lover, I come to Your door.
Place my hand on the latch
And enter.
I have been here before
And I am not disappointed.
Lord, I feel You touch my soul —
Yet another wound is healed,
Seared by the touch of Your Hand.
Deep within You restore my soul.
My heart pounds and all breath is taken away.
The sweetness of Your Touch
Is greater than the consummated bliss of the marriage bed.
Here I am complete,
Made perfect by the mystical touch of the Lover,
My Lover who touches the core of my being.
Are there still greater depths to travel?
I would rest here, or journey further
But the call of the world beckons me away.
I taste the nectar of our parting kiss —
The kiss of two souls entwined in passion.
This fires my soul to believe,
To believe that, though painful,
Your perfecting Work
Is being fulfilled in my life.
There is no other feeling like this —
A perfect peace and a certainty that You are there
Whatever befalls!

Prayer & Contemplation: *Come to the door of your Lover today and simply meditate on His beauty. Take time to rest in His presence and enjoy a moment of Spirit-to-spirit intimacy.*

DAY 51

Song of Songs 3:6-8 (NIV)
Who is this coming up from the wilderness like a column of smoke, perfumed with myrrh and incense made from all the spices of the merchant? Look! It is Solomon's carriage, escorted by sixty warriors, the noblest of Israel, all of them wearing the sword, all experienced in battle, each with his sword at his side, prepared for the terrors of the night.

If it was not in the desert this would be a splendid, heart-touching and moving sight. It would fill me with awe and anticipation. The perfume increasing with each step of approach would stimulate my senses, and all my faculties would be heightened with expectation. Later we read this is how the Beloved felt...

However, like in this verse, I find myself in the desert, and therefore if I can see this happening then I watch it from behind in sorrow and grief. Frustration wells up! Why can't I be the one waiting and not the one remaining? The desert is a cruel place; why else would Solomon be escorted by fighting men? My eyes read the words "prepared for the terrors of the night", and the sense of foreboding that pre-empts such preparation wraps itself around my soul. The encroaching emptiness devours another section of me, and my hollow scream for help yet again appears to fall on deaf ears. I am left – helpless and unprotected – to face the desert... There is no hope of erotic fragrance, just the smell of arid dryness and the stench of my own body; no sound of horses hooves and the trumpet of the herald, just the eerie silence of nothing and the distant circling of vultures; nothing to touch except the grit of the desert where each grain of sand feels like a boulder. I am wrapped in the blanket of stifling heat by day and the rigid freeze of the night air. I breathe, therefore I must still be – but all my senses question even the validity of that statement.

In the desert of no relationship the easy path is the one that believes all this is futile: "Stop! Give up! Curl up! Die!" This battle to survive seems wearisome. In the day I try to look above the sand, but the sun is too piercing for that and my eyes are forced back to the sand or shut! By day I struggle to open my eyes; even that effort is energy-sapping – the coldness of nothing making the attempt seem hopeless.

I feel without hope and yet I hear words of hope – others know what it's like to be in my desert. I am tempted to shrug my shoulders and doubt – that would be the norm. No-one could know this place! No-one is me and no-one's been here!

Prayer & Contemplation: *Today's Bible verse describes Solomon and his entourage – all the richness, splendour, pomp and power. Solomon made his carriage; Solomon trained his fighting men; Solomon commissioned the workers. What have you made, trained and commissioned in your life in order to protect you? Will you trust your Lover alone today to guard your life?*

DAY 52

Song of Songs 3:9-10a (NIV)
King Solomon made for himself the carriage; he made it of wood from Lebanon. Its posts he made of silver, its base of gold. Its seat was upholstered with purple, its interior inlaid with love.

I ponder the words "with love" and "interior inlaid". This gift of love was most likely only ever seen by Solomon – a gift for the eyes of only one person. There is a sense in which it doesn't matter what anyone else thought of it, just as long as *he* responded to it. It was a gift to be enjoyed only when shut away inside and when his focus was inside and not on what was going on outside.

Soon we will move on to the Lover's description of the Beloved's beauty. There will be new depths to be found there. But first the desert must finish its work, or we will miss the new joys ahead. There are many internal vows we can make, which keep us from God's potential joy: never to be helpless again; never to need anyone again; to take the blame for allowing oneself to get into such a place of need. We can internalise that there must be something wrong with us to have such needy passions, or that if we cannot meet both our own and everyone else's needs then we are useless. Remind yourself of the old joys when you are in the desert, for in their remembering you may well find the courage to endure. You will need to endure the terror of dying: dying to all the familiar, tried and tested ways of relating; dying to all the safe, secure ways of the giving of yourself.

Prayer & Contemplation:

"Lord, I would like to overlay my interior with purple and lavish comfort. I melt inside at this prospect. The interior of Solomon's coach must have been luxurious – sumptuous, a place of softness and gentleness, a place to sink and just be – warm, safe, pure. I don't always feel like that. Yet I consider Jesus who endured... Enduring, for Jesus, was a sacrificial choice because He could anticipate the coming joy. Lord, I choose to absorb at a deeper level the godly goal of 'doing the best I can with the resources available'. Often the resources available are the weak, untried, fallen human resources within me. Sometimes I don't know what is the best because I won't even acknowledge that I have any resources! Can this desert blossom? Yes, a garden lives, dies and is reborn every day."

DAY 53

Song of Songs 3:11 (NASB)

He made its posts of silver, its back of gold and its seat of purple fabric, with its interior lovingly fitted out by the daughters of Jerusalem. Go forth, O daughters of Zion, and gaze on King Solomon with the crown with which his mother has crowned him on the day of his wedding, and on the day of his gladness of heart.

The daughters of Zion had lovingly inlaid the interior of Solomon's carriage. What do we inlay over the interior of our soul?

Solomon was wearing the crown that his mother had crowned him with – not his own crown but one given. Where does my crown come from? Am I crowned with a crown given by my mother? Has that which goes on in my mind been given by my mother? Our heavenly Father has a different crown to give – a crown of life. It is not earned but freely given.

As I read all this, there is deep sadness in my heart. There is such a deep ache in me that it overwhelms any hope of joy. I know I must run after Jesus, but my feet feel set in clay! Chained even by experience, terror surrounds on every side. I know He will not hurt me or destroy me, but with so much terror at every turn I feel trapped in one spot – and it can seem like the one spot where He is not! Am I going round in circles and slowly digging myself a deep circular grave? It is time to move from the desert verses in Song of Songs 3 and into the Lover's song of Song of Songs 4...

Prayer & Contemplation: *Do you feel that God is distant? Do you feel crowned by negative words spoken into your life? Do you long to have goodness overlaid over your soul, yet only see pain? Thank Jesus today that He will not leave you nor forsake you. Thank Him that He will lead you through the desert and into the place of new joy. Prepare your heart for His words as we look at Song of Songs 4.*

DAY 54

Song of Songs 4:1a (RSV)
Behold, you are beautiful, my love, behold, you are beautiful!

When Scripture says something once you listen hard, but when Scripture says something twice in quick succession you really sit up and take notice! We're very good at observing that when it is a promise, less likely to observe it when a command, but I wonder how good we are at receiving it when it is our Lover telling us of our beauty?

Having spent the last half of chapter 3 feasting our eyes upon the beauty, splendour, power and majesty of Solomon in all his glory, could there have been anything with more earthly qualities? Here we join with the Lover as he gazes in sheer wonder at the Beloved; my remembrance of Solomon pales into insignificance with what the Lover is feasting himself upon.

In Western civilisation we are bombarded in all our senses with man's definition of beauty, which seem to change with each new advertiser's exhortation for the new product being marketed. I wonder if any modern day advertiser would choose any of these words and images to convey beauty to fill the insatiable public desire for greater excellence. Some might, some not! Interestingly even the Lover can only compare the Beloved to created things – today things haven't changed. Yet, as we enter the depths of this description, we come face to face with inner beauty, still created by God but not so obvious; it's reached only in relationship as one soul dares to reach into another. There is revelation here that takes the breath away, even in these few words of opening utterance. Hear the Lover become speechless and full of wonder as he begins to contemplate attempting to describe not just what his natural eyes see but also what the 'eyes of his heart' see!

I can almost hear the deafening silence that is full of awe as he stands amazed, struggling to formulate words that describe all his senses are telling him... and there, like an uncorked bottle of champagne, it all fizzes out, simile after simile, each one seemingly more profound than the other and each one falling miserably short of expressing all he wants to say. I can hear the frustration welling in me for I too know that words are not enough... Mix tender actions into the recipe and the frustration becomes almost worse because the sheer vastness of all that is seen and felt defies description! Standing in the place of vulnerable nakedness, the longing to be totally abandoned into the soul of another is all-consuming, but within our mortal bodies we are trapped in fallenness which does not allow such consummation... yet! Inside, the longing groans for that time when we will be one with the Lover of our souls. Torn in the pain of our fallenness we await with all-consuming longing for the time when our reunion with our Creator will be complete.

Prayer & Contemplation: *Listen to these words again from the Lover. They are God's words of adoration towards <u>you</u>. Ask Him to reveal to you the beauty that He sees within you.*

DAY 55

Song of Songs 4:1b (RSV)
Your eyes are doves behind your veil.

The Lover is feasting on all that the Beloved is. As I've pondered how much I've missed Jesus' eyes these words tell me that He has missed mine! Inconceivable – that in all the many millions of pairs of eyes that look to Him, He should miss mine. In the Song of Songs story the Lover has eyes for no-one else and 'tis true Jesus has eyes for no-one else but me. (Not in an exclusive way, by shutting out all other eyes but in an all-inclusive way that makes each person unique and special, so that all others will be missed too.) As I find rest in His eyes so He finds rest in mine – mind-blowing! The Saviour of the world searches for my eyes that He might find rest!

Eyes like doves! Doves mate for life, and the imagery of the Lover's and the Beloved's eyes is one of wedding for life. Being always transfixed and beckoned by each other's gaze speaks of the deep satisfaction that can be found in pure love between two souls. For the entrance to the soul is through the eyes. How important it is that we should feed our eyes on the pure, the lovely; remembering that purity and loveliness are soul characteristics and not bodily outworking. We already know that the Beloved is ashamed of how she looks; sin has left its outward mark on her. To the Lover such outward markings are nothing when he is allowed access to the deep beauty of her soul.

Close your eyes and you can imagine the Lover's face alight with wonder. Draw close and hear the shallowness of His breath and realise that such soul-beauty moves Him to internal stillness. Sense Him reaching out His words to touch the fragile delicacy that stands before Him. He is totally smitten and completely unaware of the natural world around Him. He is roused in all His senses and the purity of His longing washes over them both. As her eyes are behind her veil, He waits for her to grant Him permission to enter those areas not yet revealed. This is tantalising in its sensuality.

The soul longing to be consummated by pure love is intense, and in my earthly struggles I make so many unwise choices that I hope will bring about the longed for consummation. I can hear frustration in this body but I have to wait patiently for Heaven for total satisfaction. Such longing keeps drawing me on and keeps tripping me up. Patience seems to be such a hard fruit of the Spirit to bear!

Prayer & Contemplation:

"Lord, Your eyes which seem to have been veiled to me for so long, now come to me like doves. The dove is the bird of peace, the bringer of hope. To gaze into Your eyes is food and drink, manna and wine. I am sustained. Transfixed by the beauty of Your soul I remain stilled – intoxicated, besotted and awed. My body finds rest. My mind fixes on its focal point. My soul is satisfied. My spirit communes. I hold my gaze in Your soul; the elixir I drink into my soul is sublime. Tranquillity! Serenity! Humility! The sound of cooing, whispers of love echo within. Love calls to love and love responds. Harmonics of the soul resonate throughout. Beauty is declared. Home! I belong! It is enough!"

DAY 56

Song of Songs 4:1c (RSV)
Your hair is like a flock of goats, moving down the slopes of Gilead.

Mount Gilead was the place where Jacob made a Mizpah or Galeed covenant with Laban, pledging to look after all the things that Jacob had cheated him of (see Genesis 31:21ff). "Remember that God is witness between you and me!" (31:50). God keeps watch!

It is also the place where Gideon invited those who trembled with fear to turn back from Midian. The Midianites were camped in the valley, and from the hillside Gideon and his three hundred men were used by God to rout an entire army.

Why does the Lover choose Mount Gilead for the descent of the goats and not one of the other mountains? Is it a symbol of victory? Of God's presence? Of God's promises? Of the display of God's power and wisdom? An allusion to a scapegoat? Probably! And for many more reasons, for no name in Scripture is without meaning and chosen for a purpose.

Goats... why goats? Was it the colour? According to the NIV study guide, the goats of Canaan were usually black, and tent curtains were usually hand woven from black goats' hair. The Lover's hair was also black.

Prayer & Contemplation: *God keeps watch over your life. Rest today in the assurance that his purposes for you are good, that his justice is perfect, and that his love is unconditional.*

DAY 57

Song of Songs 4:2 (NIV)
Your teeth are like a flock of sheep just shorn, coming up from the washing. Each has its twin; not one of them is alone.

Eyes, hair, teeth! Why this order? Could it be that as a man inspecting animals for purchase these would be the parts he would instinctively be drawn to? The health and condition of the animal would be revealed in these three parts. Eyes that are clear and bright, brimming with life. A clean, glossy, full coat. Teeth, all there, clean, free from decay and tartar.

Her teeth like shorn sheep – clean and sparkling! How she must have smiled for him to focus on them so sharply and to observe their completeness and identical nature! What must that smile have said? "Welcome! I am thrilled to see you! My joy is complete!" Did *he* smile to instigate such a response? I think so! I can't think a stern approach would have elicited a smile to reveal the teeth so fully. Was it more than a smile? A full laugh, head thrown back in sheer delight – with a whoop of glee?

'Sheep' and 'twins' – to any shepherd for a ewe to produce twin lambs would be his delight for it would double his profits at little extra effort to himself. It would be his hope, and he would probably be disappointed if only a single lamb was dropped.

"Not one of them is alone" – ironic that the Lover should almost immediately use an emotion word to someone who knew how desperate it was to feel like that. Would the Beloved's soul and heart warm to a man who noticed that her teeth were not alone? With all her heart she had yearned never to be alone again, and his presence with her admiring her meant that maybe for the first time in a long time, or even a lifetime, she felt special; she knew what it felt like *not* to be alone. Just as her teeth belonged in pairs, so *she* belonged; they were a pair together.

Prayer & Contemplation: *You have a place of belonging in the Father's house, in the Father's kingdom and in the Father's plan for history. Ask Him to give you greater understand of whom He has made you to be, of where you perfectly fit.*

DAY 58

Song of Songs 4:3 (NLT)
Your lips are like scarlet ribbon; your mouth is inviting. Your cheeks are like rosy pomegranates behind your veil.

If the veil covers the top half of the head it stands to reason that the Beloved's mouth will be the most open, prominent and revealing part of her facial anatomy. Would this be the only part of the surface of her skin revealed, apart from her hands and feet? Quite probably.

As the Lover feasts his eyes on those parts of the Beloved revealed naked to his eyes it is no wonder he is so observant about teeth and lips. The rest of her has to be left a little to his imagination – imagination fired by love that overflows in such exuberant and lavish wonderment.

Close your eyes and you can imagine the Beloved's lips dancing and curling like two scarlet ribbons, weaving patterns that seduce the Lover to draw close and taste the delights He so desires. Her lovely mouth becomes a welcome echoing caress of love that holds so much promise of further caresses to be explored, enjoyed and owned.

Her temples are like pomegranates. The fruit is olive-yellow with ripening red; full of sweet, luscious, juicy seed pods; tempting to the taste buds; moreish. It has the potential for fruitfulness, such seed power held within one fruit.

The temple is the place that protects the most delicate parts of the brain. In Middle Eastern culture the women would not have been considered as having brain power. But the Lover is offering to the Beloved the acceptance that she has knowledge and potential for it, and therefore the potential for more than just equality of mental status. He longs to know her, not just in her sexual beauty but in her intellectual beauty too.

The life of the Beloved is being restored. With each word that drops from the Lover's lips she is growing, standing tall, erect, open. The crying, fearful, snivelling self is being dealt death blows as love reaches into her soul's woundedness and breathes life. Love courses through her and worth causes her to bloom.

To the parched soul He has already said enough, but He continues until she is satiated. To take the Lover's words to the

Beloved and receive them as Jesus' words to me has the same effect. Lavish grace brings love's touch to my thirsty, bleeding, wounded soul. I am filled. I am full. But my soul-cry is, "Don't stop! More, please!"

Prayer & Contemplation: *Do you desire to be filled with the love-words of Jesus today? Will you receive a greater measure of His Spirit? Cry out to Him, "More, please!" He promises to give good gifts to those who persist in seeking Him.*

DAY 59

Song of Songs 4:4 (NIV 1984)
Your neck is like the tower of David, built with elegance, on it hang
a thousand shields, all of them shields of warriors.

The Lover is obviously charmed by what he sees; the use of the word 'elegance' suggests an expression of curves and slinkiness, movement that is lithe and even seductive.

Can the Lover physically see the Beloved's neck? A tower is straight and erect. But where and what is the tower of David?[11] Do shields refer to her jewellery? Probably! To the Lover the shield of a warrior is a sign of victory; a warrior would not surrender his shield (his protection) without being vanquished. For him she is the conqueror. All his senses are totally won over.

There seems little doubt of the feasting that is going on. The Lover is totally gorging himself on every physical facet of the Beloved. Interestingly he starts with her eyes, the gateway to her soul. He uses language to articulate what his physical eyes can see – but what has he seen in her soul? We catch glimpses later in the narrative, but they can only be glimpses for the soul defies descriptive language. She is known in feelings of love that are wordless. Nothing in our humanity is able to coin a phrase which goes anywhere near the breath-taking beauty of a naked, yielded soul.

The Beloved's eyes are behind a veil. I wonder if that is a physical veil, or if it's an emotional/spiritual one too! Having been so badly rejected and abused she will find it desperately difficult to unveil her eyes and allow anyone access to the depths of her being. In the allegory of Jesus and me, only He could totally come behind the veil and completely know me – but even He will wait for me to choose to remove the veil.

Prayer & Contemplation: *Once again, ask the Father to show you if there are veils over your soul. Ask His forgiveness for the things that have hidden your heart from Him, and invite Jesus to lift the veils.*

---

[11] cp. 7:4. The tower of Lebanon looking toward Damascus.

DAY 60

Song of Songs 4:5 (RSV)
Your two breasts are like two fawns, twins of a gazelle, that feed among the lilies.

The Lover's eyes caress the Beloved as they course down her form like water flowing from an unending stream. Is this fertile imagination or are they naked together? Whichever, the Beloved has eyes for nothing and no-one else. Again the youthfulness of the Beloved is highlighted in the choice of description. Even as his eyes feast, the sensuality is reaching more than just his sight. He feels the softness of her flesh in its most tender and life-giving place. Nestled against her clothing he imagines youthful fawns with soft fur enjoying the experience of browsing in the newness of their surroundings.

As Jesus draws closer to our souls we can enter into the fullness of our gift of sensuality. He browses in our depth, and we do in His. With the tender touch of love's eyes our wounded souls are restored. The lies that we have believed for years about how useless, worthless and failing we are, are swept away in His passionate gaze. At the moment of soul-touch there is no-one else Jesus would rather be with. We are perfect to Him and in Him. We are chosen – but not chosen to the exclusion of others. This is an inclusive choosiness where one-upmanship has no place and pure equality reigns. Our soul is made perfect in Him, and no apparent outward blemish can destroy that. In finite thought this is inconceivable; we cannot but compare. We live completely in a world where comparisons are made – voiced or perceived – and we live condemned that there is always someone better in one facet of life than we are.

In the melting of souls into perfection in Him we enter the eternal dimension of life in the temporal and we find mystery that is inexplicable. Yet as we enter the mystery, receive it in faith, we discover that this competitive need to strive to be better falls away. We find our hearts longing for the day when the rat race ends and we will all live in the mystery of perfection, equality and beloved-ness.

Prayer & Contemplation: *Receive healing to your soul today as you meditate on Jesus' lavish and unconditional love.*

DAY 61

Song of Songs 4:6
Until the day breaks and the shadows flee, I will go to the mountain of myrrh and to the hill of incense.

In 2:17 the Beloved has expressed her desire to stay with the Lover through all the hours of darkness and seclusion, and now we find the Lover echoing the longing. Once day breaks it is time to work; in the natural order of diurnal life, once the sun appears labour beckons. Nocturnal togetherness is so profound that there are echoes of desire that would wish day never to break.

2:17 reveals the Beloved's heart's desire to experience all the dynamism and fertility of the love, to live in his active passion. Today's verse brings the culmination of the Lover's explorations of the Beloved's form to the secluded heights of longing passion. His response is full, lavish and intoxicating. Myrrh and incense – two of the most aromatic of spices – are the images he uses to reveal his desire. The myrrh and incense are not in small measure; rather there is a mountain covered with myrrh and a hill with incense! Every sense is at the point of complete excitement. The Lover, drunk with love, finds himself almost at a loss for words.

In twenty-first century terms it may be easier to imagine the Beloved as oneself responding to Jesus the Lover with such desire – but to start in the place of being the recipient of such total consuming passion finds me completely in awe. Like the Beloved I see every reason why Jesus should want nothing to do with me, which makes the immensity of the Lover's passion even greater! I am silenced by such love. A whispered "Why?" echoes in my soul yet remains unvoiced. Grace is so much beyond my ability to comprehend that the lack of comprehension becomes a barrier to receiving all the Lover offers. I come with my thimble and He longs for me to stand under the waterfall. However, He will fill whatever I am able to bring!

If the mountain of myrrh and the hill of spice are the Beloved, then I must be so fragrant too in Jesus' life. If the Lover comes to the Beloved's breasts as mountains and hills filled with myrrh and incense and receives such gifts from her life, then can the Lover come to me, to my life-giving breasts and find such gifts? I stand back again and reason that there must be so little to find, until I stand in the place of realising that in Him I have fullness and from that fullness all can find life. In the erotic sense that is reserved for only one, but in the spiritual sense I have sustenance for all, for Jesus in me is all the sustenance any will need. Maybe it takes a woman to realise the significance and depth of life sustained by another life. In the natural realm all I had to do to feed and nurture my daughters was to physically eat myself. Within my God-created-ness what I ate became translated to what they needed. So it follows that within my God-centred-ness what I feast on in Him becomes what others need.

The Beloved becomes more beautiful and attractive the further the adoration progresses. It may be that the Lover is finding more and more courage to speak what He sees, but equally as the Beloved is adored so she will be responding to that love by physically changing and revealing more. Meet someone whose eyes are down and whose step is heavy, speak encouraging and personal words to them, and they will depart with head held higher and maybe a spring in their step. No wonder as we enter the next verse the Lover is totally besotted...

Prayer & Contemplation: *What has Jesus been teaching you? How have his words sustained you? Pray and look for the opportunities to share these things with others – to pass on the spiritual food that Jesus has fed you with.*

DAY 62

Song of Songs 4:7 (NIV)
You are altogether beautiful, my darling; there is no flaw in you.

She is *altogether* beautiful – completely, totally, absolutely – and to re-emphasise he repeats it in the 'negative positive' form: *no* flaws. If we reflect back to chapter one and all the flaws the Beloved saw in herself, we can be tempted to raise the old adage about love being blind! Is love blind? Or is it rather that love transforms the negative and the flawed? Maybe both. That has got to be good news to the Beloved! It has got to be the best news to us too! For it brings hope which is so necessary for our survival. "Where there is no vision, the people perish."[12] The Beloved had lost vision; she saw before her a hopeless life of enslavement to her brothers and continuous destruction of who she was. In the twinkling of the Lover's eye hope is restored, and where there was nothing but the stench of death, the Beloved has entered the fragrant perfumed hope that love's promise brings. With the tender touch of body, mind and soul she has been reborn and life heralds hope – hope that she will now be loved, valued and secure.

As I stand before the gaze of the Lover of my soul I offer my dirty, soiled rags of my existence, and I watch as love rushes past them and touches who I am in my soul, and life courses through *all* of me. The beauty revealed so far is nothing compared with the revelation to come. If we sense we have intruded on this relationship thus far, be breathless as we enter even further. Tread softly for you may tread on your own hopeful soul. New life is springing up, and a softness of tread and touch is required, for such life is tender and fragile. Others have already scuppered previous attempts at growth into new life by marching through in hobnailed boots. Pop on your slippers, or skip bare-footed! We will soon enter the central part of the Lover's garden – and you will be amazed!

Prayer & Contemplation: *Jesus not only sees us as pure but also transforms our lives to become so. Thank Him for His work today!*

---

[12] Proverbs 29:18 (KJV)

DAY 63

Song of Songs 4:8 (NASB)

Come with me from Lebanon, my bride, may you come with me from Lebanon. Journey down from the summit of Amana, from the summit of Senir and Hermon, from the dens of lions, from the mountains of leopards.

Having exhausted his effusive descriptive narrative, the Lover springs into decisive, pleading action. He is encouraging, even demanding, a response from the Beloved. He describes her as His bride; is this in the future or the present? This is the first time he addresses her so. Whether in just thought or in deed, it is obvious that in his mind he has determined that she is the one for him. The repetition emphasises the strength of his emotions and his request.

In modern reading of Scripture it is hard to divorce modern realities from historical and cultural ones. Lebanon is not a country as we would know it (although it may have been in some readers' lifetimes) but rather a district, an area, which during the course of Biblical history was ruled by varied nations. Geographically it contained Mount Hermon – the highest mountain of the region – which has three peaks, of which Senir is the highest. In the chronological time scale thus far it is mainly noted for being the place of Baal worship – its highest point containing the most sacred shrine of Baal.

The mention of lions' dens and mountains of leopards, both hunters and carnivores, suggests the Lover wants to steal the Beloved from the clutches of those who would seek to devour her soul if not her body. Knowing the problems of slavery she has already faced with her brothers I can hear the Lover sounding the clarion call to freedom with these words.

In the imagery of Jesus and the church, the longing for believers to be released from oppression and captivity is the central call of Jesus' ministry on earth. We read in Luke 4 Jesus' declaration that He was the fulfilment of the prophecy given by Isaiah in 61:1-3. Everywhere He went Jesus sought to bring freedom, and here we find the Lover living from the same standpoint. Such is his love that he cannot bear the thought of His Beloved remaining ensnared, neither can he risk her remaining there that she become ensnared again.

There is almost a cry of desperation in the Lover's words – a deep feeling within him that the Beloved might refuse his request. He will not insist, indeed he cannot, but the sense of urgency rings through his plea. He can see the folly of her situation. He can hear the myriad of voices clamouring for her attention – so many perverting the truth. Will she respond and go with him into the unknown, or will she choose the apparent safety of the familiar? I sense he is uncertain as he pours out more of his heart. He enters such descriptive narrative that one is left convinced that she will follow. He takes the risk of opening his soul even further to her by telling her who she is to him – not just a description of her physical attributes being likened to possessions of worth, now he reveals himself in all his soul-nakedness to her. This is vulnerability, for to be rejected after such revelation can only lead to soul-death... but love is so great that he considers her more than worth the pain!

Jesus considers the same when He looks at us. The world looks on the outward appearance, but God looks on the heart; so God said to Samuel, when Samuel was looking for a new king for Israel. That remains true. Beneath every tough, weak, arrogant exterior there lies a wounded, bleeding soul that needs to hear its Creator speaking these words and pouring out His soul for it. Enter the next few verses with openness. Make yourself comfortable, relax in yourself and open your soul to the truth of who you are. Resist the temptation to dismiss these words as being spoken to another. Jesus, Lover of your soul, has eyes for no-one but you as He utters these sublime love-words. Reach into the truth of His soul and look into His eyes of love, for in so doing you will find barriers, fears, and wounds melting in the avalanche of love that awaits. Jesus does not want you to stay where Baal is worshipped; He longs for you to descend to the plain to rest by still waters, in green pastures... He is in the business of restoring your soul.

Prayer & Contemplation:

"I tune in to Your Spirit's voice within and hear the same echo: 'I came to bring freedom to the captives.' I hear You rejoice in me for the freedom won in my spirit and soul, and I rise up in response to bring the same freedom to others who remain snared."

DAY 64

Song of Songs 4:9 (NIV)
You have stolen my heart, my sister, my bride; you have stolen my heart with one glance of your eyes, with one jewel of your necklace.

Again repetition highlights for us the strength of emotion in the Lover's soul. I was going to write, "heart," but it's been 'stolen' – the emotion must be emanating from elsewhere. The Beloved's use of the word 'heart' is tongue in cheek – and yet we often interchange heart and soul as if they were one and the same! The KJV uses the word 'ravished' for 'stolen'. The Lover is emphasising the totality of his absorption into the Beloved. Every physical part of him is disturbed and touched by her. Every mental part is filled with her. Every emotion is set on fire by her. He is consumed! For only the physical to be touched, he would find himself eaten by lust, and probably the word 'ravaged' would be better suited than 'ravished'. His longing is to give to her all that he is. Lust would seek to take and use. Love always seeks to give. With his words he is lavishing upon her as much as he can.

Jesus does as much to us. The fact that the Lover has to repeat himself and keep telling the Beloved how he sees her suggests that she is finding the description hard to receive – not surprising really, bearing in mind the low self-esteem and abuse she has suffered. There is a sense in which the Lover is offering the Beloved all she ever wanted. We have heard her soul-cries as she has searched in vain for him, and now that potential is there for her to have all she desires and more she finds herself unable to receive what she's hearing. Behind his words I can hear the voice of self-contempt in her mind undermining all he is saying – diluting his passion to a point where she considers it a lie. "He doesn't really mean it. After all, if he knew about XXXX he wouldn't be saying that." Self-contempt is desecrating everything and pouring scorn on the fire of passion. She is in grave danger of putting out of her life forever the one thing that her heart desires.

Whether the Lover realises that I don't know! Maybe all these words just keep tumbling from his lips with no pause for the response; maybe he senses by looking into her eyes that she is struggling to receive, and so he continues to heap lavish praise in every effort to convince her of the truth of what he sees and the honesty of his passion.

One glance of her eyes is enough for him to see beyond all the barriers of self-protection and catch a glimpse of the beauty of her soul. He is able to look past the rubbish, the pain, the wounds – and their souls touch. One glance is enough to convince him that she is all he needs, but there remains the job of convincing her.

Prayer & Contemplation: *What word of encouragement has Jesus been repeating to you? Will you choose to accept that He sees you as you really are? Talk to Him about this.*

DAY 65

Song of Songs 4:9 (NIV)
You have stolen my heart, my sister, my bride; you have stolen my heart with one glance of your eyes, with one jewel of your necklace.

I find it hard to believe that I could be the Beloved of Jesus. I can point to so many others who are more deserving than I of such an accolade! Maybe that's why I can imagine how the Beloved is feeling the Lover's passion so hard to receive, for I find myself doing as much to Him! I want to do something to be acceptable to Him – to earn the right to have Him lavish praise on me. But grace does not work like that! Even when I am in one of life's pigsties He still speaks to me using words like the Lover's. How can I have stolen Jesus' heart?

Then I ponder Calvary; I come to the foot of the Cross and feel Love's blood washing me clean – and I *know* I have stolen His heart. To steal suggests I have taken illegally; but in His grace it is freely given. The worst I can do is to refuse the gift! Refusal, rejection – what further pain that would inflict! At the foot of the Cross I hear Him whisper, "You have stolen my heart, my sister, my bride, with one glance of your eyes!" I cry out to be able to give Him more than a glance – but in the anguish and suffering that confronts me, one glance is all I can face. Love's pain beckons me on. Love's whisper draws my heart strings, for never have I heard such beautiful words. Never have I, in my wildest imaginings, dreamed such abundant love was possible. I melt inside; self-contempt is subdued, silenced. I stand – no, I lie down – in awe, totally overcome by the power of love.

Reason grapples with soul experience and loses the battle. There is no reason why the Son of God should be with me speaking in soul-whispers. In my effort to reason I risk closing Him out. The effort to reason takes so much mental and emotional energy that there is nothing left for Him. But I cry, "Choose my soul! Choose my mind!"

Prayer & Contemplation: Find a comfortable spot. Cease your struggle with reason and lie down in green pastures. Let Your Lover restore your soul. Feast at the table He has set for you. You may be surrounded by many enemies but one glance of your eyes into His will assure you that love is everything you need.

DAY 66

Song of Songs 4:10 (NIV)
How delightful is your love, my sister, my bride! How much more pleasing is your love than wine, and the fragrance of your perfume more than any spice!

With overuse so much of our vocabulary loses its depth and charm. 'Delightful' is one such word. We can easily skip the word because of its seeming insignificance. But let's stop and unpack what the Lover is saying.

Delightful = Delight + ful.

The 'ful' is what it suggests: full! Not just measured to the mark or to the brim but overflowing; not just trickling over but gushing non-stop. There is an exuberant life flowing through this statement.

Delightful = De + light + ful.

I'm not sure that the etymologists would break the word up like this, but as I enter into the depth of emotion that this statement brings I find my soul flooding with light, and I sense the same happening with the beloved. The 'light of love' has a unique way of entering the imprisoned soul, and even if the body is physically caged the light makes the bars fade to nothingness. This light is the 'light of life' to her; it enables her to see a dimension of who she is that (if she's ever seen it before) has long since been forgotten. As the Lover reveals the passion in his soul, He brings the 'light of revelation' that tells her that she is not dark, depressing, useless and of no significance. Love sweeps all that rubbish away, and with the dawning of light comes the hope that she can be different.

Prayer & Contemplation: *You are the light of the world. How does Jesus' light touch and transform your soul? Pray that His light will transform others through you.*

DAY 67

Song of Songs 4:10 (NIV)
How delightful is your love, my sister, my bride! How much more pleasing is your love than wine, and the fragrance of your perfume more than any spice!

Listen with your soul and you can almost hear the Beloved rise after having been weighed down with so many cares and worries. Listen again and you may hear Jesus speaking these words to you. If you don't, keep coming to this place *for He is speaking.* He is speaking to *you* – not words of judgement that you may think and believe you deserve but words of lavish love, affection and forgiveness. The Lover has caught a glimpse of the love in the Beloved's soul. She has opened the windows of her soul long enough for him to drink enough of her love to be intoxicated by it. In her, this king, this Lover, has found something all his riches and skills could not buy or work for. It is her gift to him. From her perspective I guess she's amazed that he should want it, let alone long to receive it – yet here he is standing in her presence, finding himself filled and full in a way never before experienced.

As the Beloved has spoken of the Lover's perfume so he now speaks of hers – more pleasing than spice. To afford spices is luxury, and to know what they smell like means he must have sampled them. Here is more lavish praise. This perfume is not applied but it is part of her being. He is entering below the surface, and all his senses are filled with who she is. As with all of us he is left to the material to try to describe the invisible. His wildest imaginings reach deep into the power of his vocabulary, but still I sense that the words on the page do injustice to the emotion he is feeling. It is so all-encompassing that no words suffice. I hear the Spirit whisper, "And that is how Jesus feels about you!" In the overflow of love I am silenced; in the stillness of my centre I float in love and spiritual consummation.

Prayer & Contemplation: *Hear love's whisper in your soul today. Know that that love is also powerful – so powerful it hurts. Don't be afraid! Don't forget! Don't flee! Rest! Listen! Open your soul and watch in awe as the Lover enlarges your capacity to be.*

DAY 68

Song of Songs 4:11 (NASB)
*Your lips, my bride, drip honey; honey and milk are under your
tongue, and the fragrance of your garments is like the fragrance of
Lebanon.*

For the Lover to be so expressive of his experience of the Beloved
he has to be talking about reality. Much of what he's described thus
far is by sight or by imagination, but the reader of these words is left
in little doubt that what he describes here is something that is
experienced. It has happened; it is something that he has actually
tasted. Imagine him standing open-mouthed receiving all the
goodness and sweetness that is dripping from her lips. Just like a full
honeycomb cannot contain the honey so her lips are luscious and full
and cannot hold back from releasing their love to him.

God told Moses he was taking him to a land flowing with milk
and honey, and the spies reported that the Promised Land *was*
flowing with milk and honey. They are always symbols of the lavish
providence that God has for His children, and here in the symbolism
of this story we find the Lover (Jesus) relishing the fullness of the
Beloved (the church as a whole and us as individuals as we enter this
intimate love relationship with Him). My limited mind finds it hard
enough to accept and receive that I am in relationship with God who
lavishes undeserved grace on me; to try to conceive Jesus, Holy Son of
the living God, receiving such from me defeats all my powers of
reason and logic! However there is a witness in my spirit of the truth
of this. Relationship that only flows one way is no relationship. As
we watch the threefold godhead relating in perfect unity we must by
faith appropriate the truth of how Jesus longs to relate to us, for only
then will we find the freedom and security to be who we are created
to be and thereby be Jesus in our communities. As I draw close to the
Lover of my soul and feel His heartbeat, I hear it strengthen at the
prospect of such faith in me, in you.

Bearing in mind all we've already observed about Lebanon and
Hermon and Baal worship, it's hard to determine whether the
description of the Beloved's garments is a compliment or not! But as
it's surrounded by so many other positives, I think we can safely

assume that its message is also positive. What does Lebanon smell like? Is there a particular fragrance connected with this place? The rafters of their house are cedars[13] so maybe the reference refers to that lingering fragrance that lasts when you're surrounded for any length of time by one strong scent. Cedar has its own fragrance, and I can imagine that if the Beloved has to descend from the mountains (probably covered with cedar trees) then the fragrance of the trees will probably linger in her clothing – aromatic, pungent, yet another dimension to the fullness of the Beloved that the Lover drinks in with all his senses. He is so infatuated that he is noticing every detail in an attempt to define and even confine the indefinable!

Prayer & Contemplation: *How is God's grace and favour seen in your life? Do you enjoy good health? A warm home? Supportive friends? Creative gifts? Above all, we all have the opportunity to be God's children and the promise of an eternal home with Him. Spend some time to thank Him today for each good thing he has given you.*

---

[13] See Day 28

DAY 69

Song of Songs 4:12a (NASB)
A garden locked is my sister, my bride...

Never has a short phrase had such a deep and profound effect in me than this verse! You see, like the Beloved, I lived an illusion, a corruption. Everything I thought everyone else expected me to be I tried. If I say so myself, I think I did a pretty convincing job! But therein lay my jail; I believed I had to be what the world and the church seemed to be telling me I ought to be. I often still believe it, and God brings me afresh to these words.

These words were His heart-cry to me; behind the words I could hear His heart's longing to know the *real* me... which in turn stirred up the deep longing in me to know Him. In disbelief I tried to run away, pretend I couldn't hear, piously say to myself, "God is holy. He couldn't possibly want to know me!" Truth is, I didn't know what lay locked behind the neatly erected barricades that protected the real, raw, naked and vulnerable me. I'd slammed the doors shut as a defence mechanism the day I had been born. It has taken long and often very painful years to realise that. Now I have to believe it and live on by exploring this 'new me' that God has unlocked.

I rebelled when God told me I was a garden. I didn't want to be a garden! After all, what does a garden do? It doesn't do anything. It just is and it has things done to it! That was not for me, thank you, God! If I was going to have anything to do with a garden then I'd be the gardener... But fairly soon God said, "*I am* the Gardener," and I want to tend the garden, *my* garden. As I listen to these words again I hear the Lover reach to the Beloved in the same way, owning His deep, deep longing to be the one who tends the garden that is her. He is standing outside the gate admiring such beauty but knowing that there is so much more to be found behind those locked gates. I wanted to believe that I was helpless to unlock the garden – that it was someone else who had locked me in – but slowly, slowly God revealed that I was the one who held the key. I had made the choice to lock up the garden, and equally I had the choice to unlock it. After much soul-searching, giving and receiving of forgiveness, I started unlocking the garden gates, and to my surprise I enjoyed and enjoy being a garden. The fears I had had, that the little garden in me would be destroyed, proved totally unfounded, and the delight of welcoming soul after soul into the garden for them to taste and see that the Lord is good is such a privilege.

Prayer & Contemplation: *Is your garden locked up? Invite Jesus in to every part today, to enjoy together with you. He is waiting!*

DAY 70

Song of Songs 4:12a (NASB)
A garden locked is my sister, my bride...

Yesterday I told something of how significant these words have been to me. What about the phrase "my sister, my bride"? For quite some time they remained just words tacked on to finish the sentence in the Lover's flowery, poetic style, but I gradually became aware that I was deliberately choosing to ignore them. On one level, they talked of a relationship with God that I considered 'blasphemous'; on another, deeper level they were knocking at the doors of my deepest longings pleading to be let in. I reasoned that it must be blasphemy to even consider God as Brother and Lover! Saviour? Yes! Maker? Yes! Lord? Yes! Judge? Of course! But the idea of a holy God being something as intimate and tender as Brother and Lover could not possibly be right. Yet the ache persisted. In fact, it more than persisted, it grew, until such time as I sat quietly, stilled myself and said, "Lord, if this is You stirring in my soul in such passionate ways then please will You come in? But if this is evil, or just me, then will You please take it right away – I want nothing to do with it." (I think the Beloved may have gone through the same process.

As I sat, He took me at my word; I became alive! I looked around, and the dying garden sprang to life as the water of God coursed through me. I realised almost immediately the difference between merely existing and actually living – understanding that I'd spent nearly forty years merely existing! Recalling those times brings back all the feeling memories – only now they are even more profound because God has moved me on and I understand more fully my state of beloved-ness. Racing on, I wanted to find out more and more about my Brother and my Lover, relationships which, in truth, I had never really experienced and still fail to experience because so much clutter gets in the way.

The Lover did not just love the Beloved because of what he could see, nor because of what she could do; he loved her for who she was on the inside – warts, flaws, faults and all. To awake to the fact that God loves me in such a way and will work to change those negative things in me (but will still love me even if I refuse to choose to change) was and is quite literally beyond my wildest imaginings. Paul, too, recognises this in his prayer for the Ephesians (chapter 3).

To walk with my intimate Lover in the garden of my soul is peerless. To watch Him tend the plants and to allow Him to weed, prune, mulch etc. is such a privilege. To see the joy in His eyes as each new plant springs to life is privilege enough – but to see Him do similar in others as they walk in my garden has to be the added bonus! "But what about the spring and the fountain?" I hear you ask. "Later!" I reply. "Let's just sit here, watch the Gardener, smell the fragrance as He brushes the plants, taste the fruits He picks and be still with Him. Here is solitude – pure relationship with the Creator of everything. Be silent."

Prayer & Contemplation: *Spend time with the Gardener today. Ask Him to help you see the work He is doing in your life. Thank Him that he loves you unconditionally and that he delights to tend to your soul.*

DAY 71

Song of Songs 4:12b (KJV)
...a spring shut up, a fountain sealed.

Recently, I heard a friend say, "Nothing I can do will make God love me more, and nothing I do will make Him love me less." I pondered about the choice I have to make. God's love remains constant but my choices do not; consequently in my choices I can do things or not do things which will stop me from *finding* God's unconditional love. I am the one who puts the conditions in the way, not Him! In the past I've made choices concerning how to use my time (from my perspective, profitably), but now I am choosing to change the focus of how I use it; I am coming aside to meet with the Person who loves me more than all the other people put together. I enter into my nothingness, my emptiness, and I sit with the One who is fullness of everything. I hear Him whisper in my soul, "You are a spring enclosed."

In my memory I revisit the time when these words hit me powerfully. I remember the violent inner struggle as I rebelled at the truth. My memory moves on and sees the transformation, and I can barely recognise myself! From my spring being shut up by fear, by me, by others, to my spring being enclosed only by God is a long, long journey. I haven't finished it yet, but I can already marvel at the changes not just in me but in so many others.

Let's go back! Why would the Beloved have enclosed her spring? Probably for many reasons, as I did. The water of life was poisoned; the world's life entered the sacred life and desecrated it. Most of us have seen still, stagnant, stench-filled water and walked away, noses held in disgust! When I believe the water in my spring is like that I will close it up because, having been abandoned once, the fear of rejection to abandonment again is to be avoided at all costs. But my choice of action, rather than making matters better, makes it worse. Stagnant water is not made fresh by sealing it further.

Listen! The Beloved talks of a spring; a spring has to have a source. That source brings hope, potential for fresh water to come and wash the stagnant away. Ignoring the putrid, the Lover goes for the potential.

Listen! Jesus does and says the same to you and me. There may be putrid, rank water with a stench to mask my perfume but He sees the hope, the potential of a channel washed clean by pure, flowing water, the waft of a perfume to flood the soul of others dying in stagnation.

Look! The pain of the present and choosing to watch as He cleans out the channels is worth the life-bringing potential that fresh water will bring. He says, "I am come that they might have life, and that they might have it more abundantly."[14] His abundance is full, free and fantastic. His love is lavish, luscious and life-giving. His presence brings peace, passion and potential. As the Lover looks at the Beloved, the water of His love is already breaking down the enclosure around the wellspring of her life. If her stooped shoulders and bowed head have not yet risen in response then they surely must now.

Prayer & Contemplation: *Is there a spring in your life that you have chosen to shut up? Do you block the flow of God's unconditional love toward you? Invite the Gardener to open up the springs. Make a decision to allow Him access to every area of your life, even those parts you may be ashamed of.*

---

[14] John 10:10 (KJV)

DAY 72

Song of Songs 4:13-14 (NASB)
Your shoots are an orchard of pomegranates with choice fruits, henna with nard plants, nard and saffron, calamus and cinnamon, with all the trees of frankincense, myrrh and aloes, along with all the finest spices.

The sacrifice required from us is to yield up that which we hold most dear. Have we a powerful enough vision of Jesus? We can struggle with a sense of unworthiness, but in putting ourselves down we actually sin. Almighty God created, designed and made all things. He knows exactly how each works and the function for which they were prepared. He knows why things don't always work properly. He knows what needs to be done to make them work again. So often it is not the symptoms that need healing, but the root cause.

Jesus knows all of the plants that grow in your garden. Perhaps the list includes calamus, the one that can heal. You have to listen to Him, put yourself in the right place with the right person and just sacrifice the calamus by allowing Him to use you by your mouth and the laying on of hands as the channel for His healing. But all the plants are equally important. Some flower and colour. This is like the teaching gift – it not just by word of mouth but by living example. So much fragrance is involved too. Just by us being with people, Jesus brings the beautiful aroma of His presence. Myrrh is used for embalming. This speaks of death – but also of moving from death to new life. It protects the body and deals with offensive odours.

Sometimes I do not ask a question about someone, for fear of being nosey. Then I realise that this cripples the relationship and keeps me closed up. I should be a perfume spread abroad by the wind. As I draw alongside people they appreciate the perfume, the fragrance, and will not be threatened.

Prayer & Contemplation:

"Lord, I see from the list of herbs and spices that are contained in my fragrance that there are ones that are not necessarily connected with pleasant experiences and yet they provide healing. Help me to take this as assurance that You will only bring this about for another's ultimate good."

DAY 73

Song of Songs 4:13b-14a (NASB)
... henna with nard plants, nard and saffron...

Henna and nard are symbols of sensuality and beauty. What about saffron? Saffron is obtained from the crocus. It is the dried stamen and cross-shaped stigma – the very heart of the flower, the major part of its reproductive system yielded up; it is laid out to dry in order to give just a tiny amount of spice. Saffron is used to flavour and to give so many things their bright yellow colour – not to mention its delicate fragrance.

How often have I stood and admired a lawn or bank full of crocuses, resplendent in the variety of flower colour... How many of them have to make sacrifice to yield such a little spice? Is it any small wonder that just a tiny amount of saffron is so expensive? The wonder of all this encompassed in my garden astounds me. The Lover drinking all this in must be feeling completely overwhelmed, washed away by love.

I wonder why the Lover links henna with both nard and saffron? Is it to do with the expense? Is it to do with the rarity? Is it to do with the sacrifice? Is it to do with the luxury? All of these and probably more! He is trying to make the Beloved understand exactly how much He loves her. No price is too much; no sacrifice too great. Time and again he mentions the most precious, the most fragrant, the most pure, the most beautiful. Superlatives flow like the river that flows from the Temple of God.[15]

Prayer & Contemplation: *No sacrifice has been too great for God to express His everlasting love towards you. He even sacrificed His perfect son, Jesus, on the cross, in order to lavish His love upon you. Ponder the enormity of what He has done for you. How does that impact your life today?*

---

[15] See Ezekiel 47; John 4; Revelation 20.

DAY 74

Song of Songs 4:14b (NASB)
...calamus and cinnamon with every kind of incense tree...

Calamus is a spice made from the dried flowers of a slender reed-like plant. It has cobweb-like white flowers with brown stamens. The stalks are hollow and used to make musical pipes. The spice is used as a flavouring but also to produce a lingering perfume.

Cinnamon is a tree with glossy, dark green leaves and white blossom. To obtain the spice the outer bark is broken away and the inner bark stripped off, curled and dried to give sweet, refreshing cinnamon sticks, which in turn are grated to make the fine powder used in baking.

The aroma of both of these lingers, and there is no doubt which spice has been used. Such sweetness surrounds the Beloved. The Lover drinks it in through all his senses.

The combination of a tree and a slender reed-like plant reminds me of Peter – strength and weakness together – and yet in storms it is more likely that the slender plant will remain standing, bending with the wind and then springing back into place when the wind dies down. Sometimes the things we perceive as weaknesses in us are the very things that hold us strong in the tough times.

Since being diagnosed diabetic, cinnamon has become a friend of mine. I never really liked spices that much. I was much more of a 'herby' person. But cinnamon is my ally, a substitute for the sweetness of the sugar now denied me. So, in reading that cinnamon grows in the garden, I understand the sweetness that it brings to the Beloved. There has been bitterness in her; we hear it mingled in with her shame as she talks of how she's been treated in chapter one. As the Lover adores her it's as if this dormant plant of her life is watered and springs to life in an instant. Where bitterness, resentment and hatred ruled, sweetness now pervades, driving out the darkness and pain and bringing light and life. Such life! Did the Beloved feel as if she was walking on air as she listened to her Lover? I ask that because as His words reach into my soul that is how I feel. As I see what potential there is in my garden I believe with the Apostle Paul, "I can do all things through him who gives me strength."[16]

Every kind of incense tree! How many are there? Too many to mention by name? Probably! They come in a range of colours, so to describe the Beloved thus suggests vibrancy about her personality – life in abundance, just as the slightest of breezes makes the leaves dance. Imagine the cavalcade produced by the wind of love as it whispers through the soul-grove: dance after dance; gentle touch and flamboyant gesture intertwined to perform a display that is more alluring and majestic than the courtship of any bird or beast; again swathed in intoxicating aroma that saturates all it embraces. Fullness and abundance ring around the Lover. Maybe we begin to perceive why love shouldn't be awakened until it desires.

Yet, there is pain in all of this – deep and wounding. For the tree to yield its precious resin it has to be cut and to bleed slowly. An incorrect cut and the tree will be disfigured or killed, but with the wisdom of years and the mentoring from former generations, the skilled worker can persuade the tree, year after year, to bring forth its promise.

We are reminded of the greatest gift ever – the Son of God as babe in a manger; growing to perfect man and crucified saviour; heralding the truth that love not only costs but is also prepared to pay the ultimate price. How often we view our suffering as punishment for misdeeds or the unfairness of God, whereas in reality we are being asked to learn to love completely. Love will carry its sweetness, lushness, beauty and potential, but it will also carry its pain, grief, agony and sacrifice, and until we come to accept that and even welcome it then we will always find love to be shallow, fleeting and probably unfulfilling.

Prayer & Contemplation: Is there an area of suffering in your life that you are struggling with? Ask God to bring His spice and fragrance from the pain, to teach you to love more perfectly, and to turn even your weaknesses into His strengths.

---

[16] Philippines 4:13

DAY 75

Song of Songs 4:14d (NASB)
...myrrh and aloes, along with all the finest spices.

Such contrast! Myrrh comes from a low thorn bush whilst aloe comes from a giant among trees. Yet such similarity! Both plants have to be wounded to release their fruitfulness. The myrrh tree has sharp thorns, and it bears crimson flowers from the ends of the thorns. Myrrh is a bled resin from an incision in the bark; so the myrrh collector has to run the gauntlet of the thorns to obtain his prize. For the plant though, this is important, for without yielding the resin the plant will not flower and potential for propagation will not occur! Paradoxically it needs to be wounded to survive.

The aloe tree is so huge that to walk beneath its canopy is like entering nature's cathedral, as the sunlight plays through the leaves and they in turn dance in the breeze. Aloe is a spice which is collected by stripping off the bark. The bark grows quickly and so aloes can be collected several times a year. The tree has a root base broader than its leaf base, and so it will withstand most of the weather thrown at it. The stripping of the bark far from weakening the tree strengthens it as it uses energy to replace the bark.

If the Lover looks low he finds precious treasure in the Beloved's garden, if he looks high the same: comfort and caring and yet the potential for pain!

Prayer & Contemplation: *Wherever Jesus looks in your life – high or low – he sees the goodness that Father God has created in you, albeit mixed with pain that the world has added. Ask Him to show you what He sees – to broaden your understanding of who you truly are.*

DAY 76

Song of Songs 4:13-14 (NASB)
Your shoots are an orchard of pomegranates with choice fruits, henna with nard plants, nard and saffron, calamus and cinnamon, with all the trees of frankincense, myrrh and aloes, along with all the finest spices.

This reads as if the Lover goes ever deeper into the Beloved's potential – starting with the easy, the pleasant, the comfortable and the acceptable... until such a point where he reaches the painful, the wounding and the sacrificial.

Left to me I would choose for the easy way – picking the fruit, enjoying the flowers, taking in the fragrance – but in His wisdom God draws me to the sacrificial, the painful, the wounding. No compulsion – at every step I can stop, I can walk away. But the fragrance of God, who is love, fills my senses, awakens my desire and asks me to choose to love Him sacrificially. I look into the eyes of the Lover of my soul, I see the love that led Him to choose such sacrifices, and I am secure. He will never ask me to endure more than I can withstand, never ask me to go in my own strength but always faithfully provide His. I rejoice in the steps I have made as He has carried me through. I sorrow at the times I have looked at my own weakness and unworthiness and have chosen to walk away.

What about all "the finest spices", I hear you ask? I think the Lover has run out of his list and in sheer exuberance leaves the choice to the Beloved. I wonder what she would have chosen and why. I wonder what I would choose and why. All I know is that they would be there for a purpose, not just for decoration, and that that purpose would be manifold. It would change my life; it would change others' lives – always for the better, for the making of all of us to be like Jesus. Choices, choices! They are always there, but so is the Holy Spirit to help us make wise choices based on godly values.

Here is one final note on what is growing in the Beloved's garden: many of the things growing are what drew her to the Lover; they are the qualities *she* sees in *him*. How much we need to see them also in ourselves and thereby be enabled to release the potential!

Our potential is a life-garden that reveals beauty and brings food, drink, colours, perfume and flavours. It anoints, heals, comforts, provides shade and shelter, and so much more – all that is needed to sustain life and to bring the love that fills life to overflowing. It cycles through receiving, growing, yielding and dying – the pain and the potential of love.

Prayer & Contemplation: *What "finest spices" will you offer Jesus from your life today, and why? Ask Him to take these aspects of who you are and to use them for his purposes – to transform the lives of others.*

DAY 77

Song of Songs 4:15 (NASB)
You are a garden spring, a well of fresh water, and streams flowing from Lebanon.

Debate arises over the first two words of this statement as to whether the Lover is still talking about the Beloved or alternatively about himself. So it may read, "I am a garden spring." Either way the words have so much hope and fruitful, life-bringing potential.

If they mean "You are…" they are a final flourish to this eloquent description that has seen the Beloved's eyes and heart rise to a place they've never been before. They bring the culmination of love that releases the Beloved from being incarcerated in self-doubt to a place of freedom – freedom to bring life to others, the Lover included. Such affirmation has broken the seals, and she is free to give of herself unreservedly for the good of all. Such also is the intention of Jesus in sending His Spirit into our locked up lives that we may be so secure in Him that we are free to give ourselves liberally away. There is water bubbling up into the garden to bring life to the immediate surroundings, washing down years of guilt and shame. The well brings life much further afield for it flows, not just a gentle trickle but a gushing stream coursing down the hillside. God is always lavish in His provision – a double underlining that the life we live is for others. Who knows where the water will flow? Watch and listen, for you never know when it will come flooding back into your own soul!

If the Lover, with these words, talks of himself as being the well and the fountain, the potential remains for the Beloved. For in joining herself so intimately with him there is, at her disposal, his fountain and his well which are inexhaustible. His water will bring life to her garden; it already has! His water will fill her emotional tank time and again. It is not an arrogant statement intended to keep her 'under his thumb'; it is a freeing statement that says, "Everything I have is yours." Whichever, this paean of praise ends with a note of promise, and holding our breath we await the Beloved's response!

Prayer & Contemplation: *Give to Jesus unreservedly in worship today, and drink from the streams of His refreshing presence.*

DAY 78

Song of Songs 4:16a (KJV)
Awake, O north wind; and come, thou south.

Since we left the Beloved exhorting the daughters of Zion to come and look at King Solomon and his entourage we haven't heard a word from her, although we have imagined her responses to the Lover's overtures. We sense the awesomeness and grandeur of what she is looking at; she has focused her attention down and down until she has eyes for only one. Eager to meet with him and to be with him and yet reticent to offer herself because of her total feelings of unworthiness, we enter her ambivalence; we wonder, even with these first few words, quite what her response will be! We long with her that she would fall into his arms, but we recognise that such negative feelings could just as easily provoke her to push him away. Even now we are left with her ambivalence. She probably believes that she deserves the north wind to blow – to come with a vengeance and wreak the havoc she believes her misdeeds are worth. Everything she has heard fall from the Lover's lips leads her to believe that he has no desire for vengeance, but so strong can self-contempt be that it can be impossible to predict its response. Hear the pendulum swing: "Strike me down! Lift me up! Strike me down! Lift me up!" In an endless ticking we wait.

Her horticultural expertise in looking after her brother's vineyards will give us some clues. She will know that the cold north wind is as vital to the vineyard as is the warm south wind. For growth, both are needed. Without the bitter cold, bugs and viruses thrive, and in its right season the north wind assists the vineyard's growth. The warm heats up both soil and air to revive the plant from its winter hibernation. Without the hibernation the energy of the plant would wither in the heat of the summer. Winter is needful to build up the energy stores.

The Beloved knows all this and brings us its interpretation to play in her response to the Lover. Love's north wind will of necessity kill off the evil desires (the little foxes?) – the bugs and viruses that seek to undermine. Love's south wind will provide growth, bring life and allow restoration to come about.

She invites and welcomes both. Love has tough things to say as well as tender, and she identifies her need for both. So must we. All too often we harangue God for the effects of the north wind of His Spirit in our lives. We shout persistently for the 'feel-good factor' to always abound. How foolish we are! The Beloved may not be academically brilliant nor financially advantaged, but in her simplicity she knows what's best. Best is the honing of the north wind and the growth of the south wind.

Prayer & Contemplation: *Which do you need from Jesus in your life right now – the north wind or the south wind? Welcome Him into your heart to complete the good work He has begun in you – however His Spirit chooses to blow.*

DAY 79

Song of Songs 4:16b (NLT)
Blow on my garden and spread its fragrance all around.

The Beloved, having recognised the need for both north and south wind to blow on her garden in order to bring about the desired growth, is now indicating what her expectations are when this happens; namely that the fragrance of who she is might permeate all who surround her, from her Lover to her friends and family. She has a deep inner longing to know and to be known. She finds satisfaction and fulfilment in being given away and being able to receive others' gifts of themselves.

I find that I struggle with this verse. I could ignore it and go on to the next verse, but to do that would deny the wind of the Spirit to be both north and south winds in the garden of my life. I wrestle with my understanding that I have God's best to share with others – especially when the 'other' is someone very close and special. I wrestle with the prophetic gift that I believe is in me and the call on my life. I wrestle with my own desires and longings. I wrestle with my need to be loved and accepted especially by other humans. I feel the cold north wind of the Spirit attacking pests and diseases (sin and temptation), and I know I cling to what I humanly experience for fear that the Lover of my soul will not come through for me. It is a question of obedience! Experience tells me that God has always come through – but not always without heaps of emotional pain first. Honesty requires I own the total dislike of emotional pain.

So the wind of the Spirit blows on me. What fragrance will be spread abroad – the incense of sacrificial, obedient love or the bitter aloes of selfish, disobedient self-protection? It doesn't look very nice written down. It looks less nice when I do some internal scrutiny!

The wind of the Spirit will blow, whatever my choice. The aroma will spread. I am wearing my 'got-it-all-together' mask, but those who know me will see only the lie. My integrity is under attack – not from some vicious external enemy but from parts of my un-submitted, fallen self.

There used to be craze for WWJD trinkets. It stands for 'What Would Jesus Do?' I don't want to answer that question for it reveals that Jesus would do what I am fearful of doing. I want to love Him, I want to be His fragrance – but at the moment I don't want to move on to the next part of the verse because I am ashamed that this battle has to be raging! I think I need to hear again, "He took all my sin and shame when He died and rose again"[17] – even this lot!

Prayer & Contemplation: *Will you allow the Holy Spirit to blow your fragrance to others around you today? It is Jesus who lives in you, so your scent is His scent! Choose to take the opportunities to open your life to those whom God wishes to bless through you.*

---

[17] 'You Laid Aside Your Majesty'. Words and Music: Noel Richards. ©1985 Thankyou Music/Adm. by worshiptogether.com Songs excl. UK & Europe, adm. by Kingswaysongs, a division of David C Cook tym@kingsway.co.uk Used by Permission

DAY 80

Song of Songs 4:16c (RSV)
Let my beloved come to his garden, and eat its choicest fruits.

She is ready for everything and anything! Having evoked the warm and the cold winds to do their job in her garden, the Beloved is trusting that the fragrance will be alluring, arousing the Lover's senses in order to bring him running into the garden to enjoy its bounty. Nothing is to prevent him from entering, not even her own fears and anxieties. We need to note that the ownership of the garden has changed hands. It is *his* garden – lock, stock and barrel; the good, the bad and the ugly – for she knows that the garden will only be made complete by his presence. Surrender echoes through these words, mingled with the deep longing to be totally consummated by another. The Beloved has made her choice, opened the garden, and in anticipation she awaits his arrival. It is the moment of union where mine becomes yours, and yours becomes mine, and we become one.

In all the frenetic busy-ness of life it doesn't take long meditating for my soul to rise up in similar response. In my exhaustion I long to be still by those quiet waters, to find rest in those green pastures and to have all my senses caressed by the fullness of my Lover's presence. Soul-thirst takes some slaking! So I must choose to rest and not rush off into the demands of the day however righteous they appear. Their voices make demands in my mind, and stillness of thought feels impossible to find. I want to laugh with joy for I feel Him near. I want to cry tears of anguish for all those demands I have not (and cannot) meet. I want to weep for myself and my own deep needs. I want to sleep. I want to dance. The relief is to know I can do all or any of them in His presence and He will join in. Sharing my sorrows, pains and joys is part of His great pleasure.

The Beloved already knows what the Lover will take for he has already voiced what he sees. For her to respond using the word 'choice' reveals she has already understood much of the sacrifice that will be required of her garden when he comes to take his fill. The invitation is open, full and free. Taste anything! Whatever sacrifice required will be made in order that his desire be met.

In my drained state I find it hard to believe that there are any choice fruits in my life. However I know my Lover's presence will make even the shoddiest of fruit worthy. My sacrifice is as acceptable to Him as the Beloved's is for the Lover.

Prayer & Contemplation:

"Lord, I sink into Your arms and find deep refreshment. Sometimes I feel so tired and weary that I cannot find any fruit to offer You. But I pour out for You the little that is left. Search the garden – Your garden in my soul – and take whatever fruit You can!"

DAY 81

Song of Songs 4:16a,b (RSV)
Awake, O north wind... Blow upon my garden.

Sometimes I wonder why I pray such prayers! They seem the appropriate response at the time, and then when He starts to answer them I have my doubts! He surely delights to answer such prayers, and consequently I am well advised to weigh them before I pray them. However, my heart usually gets the better of my mind. In retrospect I know that this can be a good thing because my heart longs after Him even when my mind is lagging way behind or, worse still, in rebellion!

The chill wind of His Spirit bringing conviction is one from which I would shelter, pulling my coat collar around my ears to shut out the whisperings of His voice! However, His voice, His word, penetrates between joint and marrow; what chance do any defences I construct have?

Prayer & Contemplation:

"Lord, please wither all the plants in my heart that are not dedicated to You nor grown by You!"

DAY 82

Song of Songs 5:1 (RSV)

I come to my garden, my sister, my bride, I gather my myrrh with my spice, I eat my honeycomb with my honey, I drink my wine with my milk. Eat, O friends, and drink: drink deeply, O lovers!

The Beloved sees the garden as hers; the Lover sees the garden as his – a real joint ownership.

In our garden Jesus is not just there to enjoy the view and smell the perfume, although He is filled by them and aroused. He invites us to come and look at the panorama of the garden with His eyes and catch the fragrance in our nostrils.

I watch! The Gardener comes to make the incisions in the myrrh tree so that He may collect the resin. Who is bleeding here? Is it me? Or is it Jesus? Or the pain of others? It is all of these! It is Jesus' garden, His myrrh; my garden, my myrrh; their garden, their myrrh. We need to leave time for the process. The pain will most likely be the waiting pain, the 'not knowing' pain. Don't walk away and say, "It's no use. Nothing is happening." For so much of what happens in gardens happens unseen. The pain is not a sign of failure; the pain is a sign of the Lover's presence. He is at work.

Jesus collects resin. He too needs spices – those which have to be dried, scraped, peeled, burned, crushed and grated. All of these are painful processes, but we need to understand the necessity of pain in our lives so that others may be healed. It will often feel as if your pain is useless, unproductive and not received. That is the prerogative of the receiver. But no sacrifice goes unnoticed by the Gardener. It will still bear fruit – but not necessarily in the way anticipated.

Prayer & Contemplation:

"Holy Spirit, I'm so glad that You've placed the owner's seal on me!

"Jesus, I need to hold Your hand and enter into the 'wordless', to see with the eyes of my heart and understand with my soul emotions. I choose to let go of my current depth of understanding and realise that there is understanding that is uncharted. I enter Your realm – the Gardener's realm – receiving Your purpose and Your understanding of the processes of sacrifice and growth.

That sounds painful and even impossible, but with You all things are possible. You are with me; Your powerful right arm upholds me.

"Lord, I look and see not flowers but countless seas of faces. They stretch as far as the eye can see. It's like I look at all those groups of people that I've shared with, only I see them en masse. I see bright eyes, tearful eyes, sad eyes, hopeful eyes and dead eyes. I watch the Spirit blow. Some flowers bend with the breeze and enjoy Your presence. Others remain unmoved, almost oblivious. Thank you for your presence in my garden today."

DAY 83

Song of Songs 5:1a (RSV)
I come to my garden, my sister, my bride...

Is this in the past or the present? Is it a completed event or the definition of the current position? How does the Beloved feel to have the one who so satisfies her in complete attendance upon who she is? In all the mishmash of pain, longings and fears, does she feel full of hope and totally alive? So alive that it hurts? So believing that she could fly to the moon if asked? Full to overflowing and yet... not full because there is always more, and hope demands growth; alive and complete in her longing and knowing there is still more, finding desire deeper than ever before imagined. Each time the Lover comes into the garden, the potential for boundary growth develops and the longing for more of him intensifies.

Yet in the pain of love and longing, how can she stand? Pain usually signals danger! Can she have too much of a good thing?

Prayer & Contemplation:

"O Lover of my soul, I sit in the pool of my own painful, deep longings knowing You are here; You have come into my garden. I hurt under the depth of Your presence, and hurt initiates feelings of panic and fear. 'What if's bombard my mind. Skeletons rattle in my closet, and I am transfixed, caught in a pincer movement of such longing and such sin, sometimes unable to differentiate between them both. I feel the pain and instinctively want to protect myself from it. But I choose to hold firm in it, in order that I may fully experience my Lover in His garden."

DAY 84

Song of Songs 5:1b (RSV)
...I gather my myrrh with my spice...

The Lover has gathered the myrrh from the garden for himself, and the spice is his too. Such is the surrender of garden to gardener that the fruits of the garden's labours belong to the gardener and not to the garden. The garden exists because the gardener determined it would. He made plans, prepared the soil, chose the seeds and nurtured the plants. It is he who worked to extract the myrrh and spice. So it is with us in the hands of our Creator; without His eternal vigilant care and provision there would be nothing to keep our lives in existence. A garden has no choice but to respond to the gardener's touch. The myrrh cannot decide it will not yield its resin. It cannot resist the gardener as he wields his tools against its trunk (except of course the defence of its thorns). Once cut it must bleed. Only good cuts in proper places will produce good resin. An inexperienced or injudicious gardener may only succeed in killing the tree.

The gardener in today's verse, however, has come and taken his myrrh and spice. For him it was a pleasant and beneficial experience as it was too for the Beloved. Love wounds but with purpose. Greed, anger and hate wound but with destructive vengeance which ultimately serves neither party with any benefit. The Lover's wounds bring life, love and sustenance, and satisfy both parties in the relationship, which in time spills out into other relationships. The benefit of such loving, sacrificial relationship never just touches the lives of those intimately and immediately involved, for from the fullness of being loved, enjoyed and accepted, both parties are able to give so much to so many others.

Behind myrrh's beautiful flower is its thorn – come close and you risk being wounded. Behind the thorn lies the potential for precious fragrance and healing – not something to be guarded, for it is only in the giving away that the resin brings life to the myrrh. Hanging on and defending against all comers only leaves the plant to poison itself. My spice plants only flourish and grow as they yield up painfully their precious gift. How true of life! Greedily keep and hoard, and we become possessive, defensive and impenetrable. Freely give and pour out, and we become open and welcoming thereby expanding our potential for growth.

As the Lover gathers his myrrh and his spice, imagine the fragrance that will surround him. It will linger to be a constant reminder to him of the surrender of the Beloved and the sacrifice of love she made to him. Also it will signal to others where he has been and indicate the potential for them to be the beneficiaries of the love he has received... for as we believe and know ourselves to be loved so we are enabled to love others. The depth of our love will contain the depths of the love we have received, so as we give away love, what we give away is not just ours but that of those who have loved us... and by God's design it has a way of returning magnified and multiplied.

Prayer & Contemplation:

"Lord, I have used the thorns of my garden to keep You and others away too often! But the sadness of this encourages me to move on in relationship. In love's vulnerability, surrendering my option for defence, I find acceptance and security beyond imagining and wish I'd not been so fearful and foolish for so long."

DAY 85

Song of Songs 5:1 (RSV)

I come to my garden, my sister, my bride, I gather my myrrh with my spice, I eat my honeycomb with my honey, I drink my wine with my milk. Eat, O friends, and drink: drink deeply, O lovers!

If the Lover is seen as Jesus and the Beloved as the church, then Jesus has come into the garden, this world. He has fully revealed Himself to us in such a way that we could begin to comprehend what love is. Myrrh is what Jesus was brought at birth, and spice was what He was brought after death. He came knowing that He would gather both myrrh and spice at His beginning and His end. Honey is one of the sweetest, purest delicacies known to man; it never goes off. I wonder if this refers to the sweetest, purest intimate relationship that the man Jesus enjoyed with His Bride, the Church. Certainly it must refer to that in relation to the Beloved in the narrative. The Lover also drank wine in the Beloved's garden; so did Jesus, many times, but in particular at the last Passover feast when He took wine and transformed it from its luscious, refreshing and intoxicating state and lifted it into the spiritual state. Each taste of wine is a remembrance of Him and His sacrificial Love.

For the Lover to gather, eat and drink all of these on the surface might seem a luxurious, fulfilling place to be, which indeed it was, but it was also painful and consuming for we always have to leave the emotional heights which must plummet us into grief and sadness, maintaining hope that we will ascend to such heights, or higher, again but never certain that that privilege will be afforded us.

To me, wine and milk joined together in such a way seem an anathema. Wine, intoxicating (and in our civilisation legally denied to minors), is linked with milk, the total sustenance of newborn babies. I see a rich blend of maturity tapped into a heart cry for childlikeness – a state we so rarely achieve, thinking so often we are too grown-up to do childlike things, whereas our Father keeps reminding us that we are His children and He longs for us to relate to Him in such a way. Yes, we are to give up *childish* ways – those petulant, self-centred, demanding attitudes that scream, "Me!" incessantly. *But* we are all dependent on our Father in childlike trust that He is faithful and just

– something we find almost impossible but which we see the Lover demonstrating in the love He offers to His bride.

Prayer & Contemplation: *Are there aspects of your life in which you need to become more childlike? Do you need to trust God more? Hope more? Be more humble? Ask Jesus to show you any areas that he wishes to work on in your heart. Confess them to Him and make a fresh start today!*

DAY 86

Song of Songs 5:1c (RSV)
...Eat, O friends, and drink: drink deeply, O lovers!

Such exhortation! How grateful I am to friends who have brought me similar exhortations! Usually at a time of emptiness, self-pity, exhaustion, their voices have risen in unison. Their song lifts my eyes, and I realise that my focus has completely drawn away from the source of my life. Often it is from their fullness of Jesus that I first am allowed to feast, mainly because I don't have the energy or the inclination to find Him by myself. "Here I am!" they say to me, "Even though I may not have much Jesus, what I have you can take." How joyful it is when such a sacrifice leads me back to the place of fullness. A shared journey into the Lover's arms always seems to magnify the person of Jesus, and somehow there is more of Him than if we'd journeyed individually. Sometimes I don't even need to hear their voices summon me; a look (you know, one of those 'knowing' ones) will suffice. It is such a risk, for in their vulnerability I could reject, refuse or even retaliate, but somehow love conquers and even in the worst of times when I reject and resent they will show me Jesus – they still offer me their very selves.

There are no guarantees, but so often when I return to the place of stillness in my Lover's arms and find refreshment then my friends, too, reap the benefits. For in finding love for myself I then have love to give. My Lover is always lavish, and His love persuades me not just to share what I receive but even to dare to give it all away, which stretches my faith to believe there will always be more, just as theirs was stretched in the first instance when they dared to give their all.

The friends must be delighted that that first piece of advice has been heeded. The Beloved has sought out and found her Lover. Their second piece of advice... will it be heeded?

What it is to be invited to eat and drink your fill! In Hebrew culture, to be invited to the meal table is more than just an invitation to share food. It is an open door into the life of the one who invites. It says, "I long for you to know me intimately. All that I am I give you." The host offers more than food and drink to maintain physical life – he offers love, care, security and significance. It is a statement of intent that he desires to meet every need the invited may have. To refuse such an invitation is betrayal of the worst sort – which is why the parable of the wedding banquet has so much more to say than we in our Western culture would normally realise.

The friends recognise that what they see developing before their eyes is firstly a deep friendship between the Lover and the Beloved and secondly an intimate love relationship. They call them friends and then lovers. The love these two share is intoxicating not just for them but also for the onlookers. I sense the friends becoming intoxicated themselves with the love that is flowing freely. They need to hear the Beloved's supplication not to awaken love until it so desires for they run the risk of falling into temptation... and probably desecrating themselves for their futures. How often have I wished that young people would heed this advice! So much is aroused and awakened in them; they succumb to the temptation under the umbrella of 'everyone does it', and in one moment they heap regret and remorse onto their shoulders – and, worse still, into their hearts.

Delight is in the friends' hearts and souls as they exhort the couple to feast with each other. There is no malice or jealousy – but is that going to stay? We will return to the friends and their feelings later, but for now we move on with the Beloved...

Prayer & Contemplation: *Come and receive from your Lover today. Worship Him and enjoy His love towards you. Day by day, seek Him until you know you are overflowing – and then let His love overflow to others around you!*

DAY 87

Song of Songs 5:2a (NLT)
I slept, but my heart was awake, when I heard my lover knocking...

Is this a dream sequence or is it reality? Is the Beloved pinching herself? Did this really happen? Where is reality and where is desire, and have these two become confused in her mind and experience?

This verse describes how I felt last night. All night long I kept singing, "Jesus, You have broken the chains." But I wondered whether I had been battling and whether the victory was won.

Each time we surrender more to Jesus, the next port of call is the battleground! But the Captain of the Lord of Hosts is there, and the merest whisper of His name brings victory. Each time we sing, "Jesus!" so another victory is won.

Our 'garden' can also be a battlefield; tears are shed and blood is spilled, but as each drop falls to the soil new life ensues. This is the Master Gardener, the Captain of the Hosts, about the work of building the Kingdom. But as we stay close and battle on, so the banks of the Jordan are reached and the double portion is ours. It is Jesus' gift to us. It releases us into service. His Holy Spirit, His Enabler will spur us on. It will mean more battles; it will mean more tears; it will mean more bloodshed. It will mean more victories and glory to Him! We can receive His "Well done!" but we should not 'rest on our laurels'. There are many more battles to fight, tears to shed and blood to be spilled.

We can drink deep from the waters of the river. It is our life source. We may feel spent and extremely tired, but there is still more work at hand, more visits to Bethel.

Prayer & Contemplation: *Will you surrender? Will you stand? Will you trust Jesus? Do you trust Jesus?*

DAY 88

Song of Songs 5:2 (NLT)

I slept, but my heart was awake, when I heard my lover knocking and calling: "Open to me, my treasure, my darling, my dove, my perfect one. My head is drenched with dew, my hair with the dampness of the night."

This verse contains the second of three pieces of reported speech (2:10-13; 7:8), the second and last by the Lover. It almost seems like a dream sequence favoured by so many romantic novelists of film makers. If the Beloved was asleep with her heart awake, did all that evolved happen or was it all a dream? Did some of it happen in a dream and the rest in wakefulness? Is her subsequent action a response to such a real desire that she couldn't distinguish between real world and dream world? As we shall see later the Lover seems to have completely disappeared – and very rapidly – which seems to suggest a dream or angelic visitation.

I think I can identify with the words, "I slept but my heart was awake." There are times when my body is giving way to sleep but my mind, soul and spirit are still active. Sometimes that leaves me unable to sleep physically and so I toss and turn. Here I believe the Beloved has found the place of bodily stillness, but her heart and mind are so full of all that she's seen, heard and experienced that they are feasting and partying on! Her emotions are entering the depth of the newly awakened desire, and she welcomes each new emotion as a child gazes in wonder at newly experienced delight – spellbound, eyes wide and full of wonder. I can just imagine all the unvoiced questions as she stands enraptured. Why? What? How? When? Which? Does? Is? Can?

As the Lover speaks, there are more emphatic phrases as the Lover seeks to be close to the Beloved. Currently there is a door between them, yet all his senses recall the memory of her, and his urgent longings are stirred up. What tone of voice does he use to speak these words? Are they a command? I think not! Are they a polite request? Again, I think not! Are they pleading? Does he think she's reluctant to give him entry? I don't know – part of her response suggests that he might know of her current physical state. Are they revealing of his own desires? Almost certainly! He cannot wait to feast his senses on all that is perfect about the one his heart loves.

The Lover says, "My head is drenched with dew, my hair with the dampness of the night." Where has he been? How long has he been out? What has he been doing? Surely he knew where she lived and could find her easily? Maybe he's been away and has travelled back overnight to be with her? Maybe he's been out walking the fields and lanes sorting out his emotions and desires – identifying his feelings and the intense longing to be with her. He has ignored all danger and comfort to himself and appeared on the doorstep.

Prayer & Contemplation: *Can you identify with this: walking and walking to a place of decision, still trembling with a little indecision on a friend's doorstep, wondering if the choice you've made is the correct one? Perhaps there is some "I wonder what others might say" wrapped up in this. How often we allow what we think others might think to determine our course of action! Ask the Holy Spirit for boldness today to do what you know is right. Thank the Father that He always sees you with eyes of love and approval.*

DAY 89

Song of Songs 5:3 (NLT)
*But I responded, "I have taken off my robe. Should I get dressed
again? I have washed my feet. Should I get them soiled?"*

I really can't believe my eyes and ears! What is the Beloved
playing at? Everything she needs and desires is knocking at the door,
and she's complaining about getting dressed again or getting her feet
dirty! Is it a sudden attack of propriety or prudishness that hits her –
pangs of conscience? How can clothes and clean feet be more
important than being with the one who fulfils her?

But wait a minute! I hear the little voice of conscience stab into
my indignation and frustration. "How many times have you chosen
the 'trivial' against spending time with the Lover of your soul?" I
start off on my reasoned argument that my circumstances are
different... but in the cold light of honesty they aren't at all. I fling
family, work, friends, church and fatigue at my Lover. I am no better
than the Beloved; as I tut and point the finger of disbelief at her I
forget that I point three fingers back at myself. From this place of
stillness I can see so clearly the foolishness of both the Beloved's and
my own choices.

Prayer & Contemplation: *How about you? Do you find 'reasons' to
avoid spending time in the presence of your Lover? Are you too busy
to simply rest in His love? Do you feel it is inconvenient to stop,
worship and adore? Choose to 'get dressed' again today, to meet your
Lover. Spend quality time with Him.*

DAY 90

Song of Songs 5:4 (NASB)
My beloved extended his hand through the opening, and my feelings were aroused for him.

'Thrust' to me implies speed, urgency and determination. The Lover longs to be with his Beloved. He makes his intentions and desires known to her. He hasn't waited politely after his knock; he is eager to be with her and is keen she understand his eagerness. The sight of his hand stimulates physical response in the Beloved – one which most of us would recognise: the pounding heart of anticipation. All that 'might be' rushes through her mind, and expectancy heightens her sense – the sight of his hand evoking memories of the rest of him that she has stored close to the surface. Suddenly in her mind's eye his fullness is there and her desires for him are completely aroused.

How often does my Lover do things to attract my attention that I should desire him in such a way? I probably don't know the answer to that, for I suspect that I often don't notice Him. I am so engrossed in 'me' and 'my activity' that I become oblivious to His advances. How sad He must be that I find so many other things more worthy of my time and energy than Him!

Prayer & Contemplation: *Do you notice Jesus' passion towards you? Or is your life too full with other things? Begin to thank Him throughout each day for each blessing He brings your way – no matter how small – and you will soon become aware of His determination, passion and longing towards you.*

DAY 91

Song of Songs 5:5 (NASB)
*I arose to open to my beloved; and my hands dripped with myrrh,
and my fingers with liquid myrrh, on the handles of the bolt.*

"I arose..." What was the Beloved doing? Sleeping? Resting?
Sitting? Whatever, she wasn't alert/ready. My mind jumps ahead to a
parable Jesus told, that of the wise and foolish virgins. One group
prepared and the other was negligent. Here is the Beloved, half ready;
preparing herself to smell nice but caught by the fact that she couldn't
get her hands cleaned quickly enough; enjoying the pleasure and the
anticipation but getting caught in the reality. This is partly what
makes me wonder if this is a 'dream-sequence', turning into her worst
nightmare – when we want everything to be so perfectly right, and yet
everything conspires against us, turns pear-shaped, and our worst
fears are realised in seeming slow-motion! I can imagine, like in some
erstwhile slapstick comedy, the increasing frustration of slipping
hands on the handle, the effort that's put in to achieve nothing. Not
only does she face the disappointment of him not waiting but the
frustration of her own stupidity and unpreparedness. I can hear her
now: "If only..." But to her credit, as we shall see in the next verse,
she does attempt to do something about it rather than sit and have a
pity party.

Prayer & Contemplation: *We don't know when Jesus will return, nor
when it will be the last day of our life. Have you prepared your heart
to meet Him? Have you stored up treasures in Heaven? Ask the
Father to help you set your mind on things above and to show you
what distracts you from your heavenly calling.*

DAY 92

Song of Songs 5:6a,b (NLT)
I opened to my lover, but he was gone! My heart sank.

Feel the sense of expectant joy and delight – relief after the frustration of hands slipping on the latch – only to enter the depths of dismay made more wretched by her already scrambled, negative thoughts. She stands in the place of disbelief and helplessness as fizzing joy plummets into abject emptiness.

You can almost hear the thud as her heart hits the floor! How many times had the Beloved hoped for love, acceptance and welcome only to find it snatched from her hands or smashed to smithereens by malicious and selfish greed? Here it was again, her worst fear realised: everything she'd ever desired so near yet so far. Can you imagine the thoughts that flashed through her mind? Or the emotions that coursed through her body? Or the pain that stabbed her already fragile soul? *Empty, lonely, gone!* The grief of desertion is so black (added to by the thought that her heart attitude may have caused him to leave) that the Beloved would be plummeting headlong into a bottomless abyss, seemingly with no possibility of return – such is grief!

The grief process is instinctive; it kicks in without invitation! "Where is he? Why has he gone? Why did I bathe now? That cursed latch!" It blames everyone and everything else. Anger rages as the desire is dashed, the longed-for goal kicked out of sight. Denial and disbelief call out, search – "Maybe I was imagining it; this couldn't possibly be happening to me! ... Okay, so it happened, but if I go looking (if I behave better, if I apologise enough, if I do penance, if I change) then maybe he'll be back...!" Sadness, that deep ache of emptiness, gnaws away leaving us a choice: revisit parts of the cycle again; resign ourselves to the circumstances and resolve to grit our teeth and soldier on come what may; reach the place of acceptance that there may be a reason for this and that ultimately God's higher purpose for us has something better in mind. One path leads to death, the other to life!

I find myself in a similar place to the Beloved in some of my own relationships at the moment – they seem very shallow. One person is distant through circumstances; time and space have just not allowed us time together. Frustration and sorrow mingle together in a depressive cocktail. Two others have been physically present but to a greater or lesser degree. Spiritually and emotionally there has been distance between us. I am fearful that the distance is of my own making.

Prayer & Contemplation:

"Lord, like the Beloved, my attitudes, revelations and withdrawals have often left me floundering, grasping for a handle that slips elusively from my grasp – physically out of sorts and scared of what might be, looking to the future and finding nothing but uncertainty and bleakness. Like the Beloved, my heart sinks. Glimmers of hope sparkle briefly but seem to no sooner be revealed than they disappear into the gloom.

"Lord, I long for You to reveal Yourself – to be there at my door. Sometimes disbelief wells up and I convince myself You wouldn't want to be there, like I'll never again be close to You. At those times it seems so long since we were close. Like the Beloved, I recognise that it's likely to be me who has driven You away. You hear the questions and remain silent.

"But I have tasted the sweetness of life, and I am compelled to taste it afresh. Lord, You have my heart. I know You have – I gave it to You! Now I will search for Your heart. I do have Your heart, but I desire it in greater measure. As You promised the Beloved so You promise me. I choose to continue the search, even when it feels painful, lonely and seemingly fruitless!"

DAY 93

Song of Songs 5:6b (NLT)
I searched for him but could not find him anywhere. I called to him, but there was no reply.

Hear the denial behind these words! "Was he really there? Maybe I was imagining. My eyes and ears deceived me. I couldn't have been so foolish as to have been so arrogant that I chased him away." She'd almost rather believe that she was seeing and hearing things than accept the fact that she'd blown it. She is frantic to believe and find him on the one hand, but desperate to believe in an hallucination on the other. Such denial tears us in two as we find reality and imagination blurring into one; we are unable to find the 'loose end' which will untangle our messed up life, only seemingly pulling at ends which tie knots and ensnare us further.

Prayer & Contemplation: *Meditate again today on being prepared for the Bridegroom's return. We can be so self-preoccupied that we either don't notice or are unable to respond to Him.*

DAY 94

Song of Songs 5:7a (NIV)
The watchmen found me as they made their rounds in the city. They beat me, they bruised me...

Not for the first time, the Beloved is off on her citywide search for the Lover. As before she meets the watchmen – friend or foe? Her first encounter suggests she might receive a sympathetic welcome. They did her no harm then. Not so this time...

Did they just physically beat her – or was this rape? We don't know! Had the Beloved fled the safety of the house in her night attire concealed beneath her cloak? In her impetuosity and desire to see the Lover, had she raced out without thought for her personal wellbeing, grabbing only her cloak for protection? Were the watchmen only after theft of property, or did they steal more than that? So often when love strikes it seems to throw away our reason and common sense, and we do the most foolish of things.

Prayer & Contemplation: *Are you so in love with Jesus that you will do the 'irrational' – not thinking of yourself but rather filled with longing to meet His desires? Find out His desires today, and set your heart on fulfilling them.*

DAY 95

Song of Songs 5:7b (NIV)
...they took away my cloak, those watchmen of the walls!

For a poor person their cloak would have been one of their most important possessions. It would serve as warmth, protection and shelter. A cloak would cover infirmities, deformities and lack of decent clothing. It would be the one item between the owner and total humiliation.

Hear the pain, the anger and the shame in the Beloved's voice – yes, physical pain from a battering and bruising, but such inner pain, emotional and psychological. They had violated her body, and that was bad enough, but they had also pierced her very self. That which was so fragile and which had been brought lovingly and painstakingly to life through the words and actions of the Lover now lay shattered at the hands of those who probably should have protected her. What abusers they were of the position they held!

Prayer & Contemplation: How often do we let the words and actions of others undermine or destroy who we are? A look, a leer, a word – they can all wreak as much destruction to self-esteem as an earthquake does to the earth's surface. In our souls the devastation can leave a landscape that resembles the aftermath of an earthquake with aftershock that can reverberate down the years. Can you identify wounds from words that need healing today? Forgive the one(s) who spoke the words, and ask Jesus what words He speaks over your life.

DAY 96

Song of Songs 5:8
Daughters of Jerusalem, I charge you – if you find my beloved, what will you tell him? Tell him I am faint with love.

In the depths of her despair and powerful longings, the Beloved again charges her friends to help her: "I charge you..." This is important, urgent even! She is pleading her case and enjoining her friends to be part of the search. What risk she is asking them to take in the light of what's happened to her! Despite her defiling, the Beloved is still set on finding the Lover.

And what is her message for him if her friends should find him first? Is it "I've been beaten up by some thugs; come and help me!"? No! Is it "Why did you run off and leave me?" No! Is it "Couldn't you have waited a few more seconds; these things take time!"? No! Her message remains filled with love: "Tell him I am faint with love!" She reminds him and herself of how she felt, that her weakness is not from her beating, nor from anger or shame, but from being in love – all those wonderful, warm sensations that bring life to body, mind, soul and spirit. Even a physical degradation cannot take away the memory, and though she may feel shame and undeserving she clings fast to the truth of the Lover's soul – that she is his and he hers! In some ways she's also warning her friends off: "I may have made a mistake in letting him go, but that doesn't mean either of us have given up on each other. Hands off!"

Prayer & Contemplation: *Are you 'faint with love' for Jesus? Do you find you just cannot help talking about Him to others? Choose to praise Jesus today through your conversations. As you do, your love will grow, and you will only want to praise Him all the more.*

DAY 97

Song of Songs 5:9 (NLT)
Why is your lover better than all others, O woman of rare beauty?
What makes your lover so special that we must promise this?

I wonder what tone of voice the friends used to utter these words. Was it a "How dare you?" tone, coming from a root of anger? Were they hurt by the Beloved's presumption that her Lover was better than anyone else's? Are they jealous? Is she shaming them that they can't find one so handsome? I suppose it will have depended on the Beloved's tone of voice as she beseeched them to help.

How often an intonation or inflection can change the meaning of our words! Sometimes intentionally so, sometimes accidentally so and sometimes subconsciously so! Often it is affected by how honest we are, and have been, with those we hold dear.

It depends on our attitude too – how we are feeling about ourselves. How do *you* read the words, "most beautiful of women"? Is it a statement of fact? Is it a comparison that leaves the friends feeling inferior? Is it sarcastic and intended to take her down a peg or two?

Whichever (and there could be many more options) it became the basis for another lyrical description of her Lover. So whether she heard that or it was not there, the Beloved is able to focus on the one her heart desires, which in turn lifts her soul away from the self-centred focus of her painful beating to love.

'Better' is a comparative, a step between 'good' and 'best'! It is often a dangerous word that causes us to feel 'never good enough'. Is there a hint of this in the friends? How many of us have been fed on:

Good, better, best; never let it rest
Until my good is better and my better best.[18]

Whilst God always gives us His best and God always *is* best, we try so hard to strive in our own strength to be the best – and when we get there it still isn't good enough because there's always more. Will it take a lifetime to realise that we cannot achieve best but we can receive best? We can be best because the Best lives in us!

---

[18] Tim Duncan

148

Prayer & Contemplation: *A thought I have found extremely helpful in my inner struggle against feeling a failure (because there is always better that I could do or be) is this: endeavour to do the best you can <u>with the resources available</u>. Living in the now, I will never have all the resources that could ever be available at my disposal because I am still growing and learning. I am learning not to live in the resignation that I could, or ought to, have done better but rather to live in the acceptance of the fact that God is still at work changing me. I am beginning to live in the freedom of beloved-ness in which failing is part of growing and 'being the best' is a relative and subjective thing; it is never absolute in human form.*

DAY 98

Song of Songs 5:10 (KJV)
My beloved is white and ruddy, the chiefest among ten thousand.

The previous attempts of the Beloved to describe the Lover have focused largely on their relationship together and how she responds to him. Here she is copying him in his use of simile to describe how he looks. Again we need to bear in mind the importance of the things she chooses to compare him with... although I think we'll have less difficulty in comprehending the value of her choices than we did with his, for many of the things she likens him to are still of great value to us today.

How easy is it to imagine ten thousand? In one sense, with modern day technology, we see pictures of crowds bigger than that beamed into our living rooms when we watch some of the great sporting occasions. It's easy to become blasé and say, "Ten thousand? That's nothing when compared to some sports crowds..." – nothing until we've actually found ourself in such a sea of humanity and then attempted to locate just one person! Would the Beloved have ever seen ten thousand? Maybe as the army marched to war! How long would it have taken ten thousand to march past? Could you pick out one person in so many? Probably not! The emphasis here is more important than the specific number; she is emphatic about how noticeable he is!

Love has a wonderful way of bringing an aura to the person beloved. We have eyes for no-one else. Her exclamation is that his aura would have made him stand out. There is no-one to touch him in aura or complexion.

Already I think of times when I have tried to describe Jesus to others. How foolish words seem, they never seem to match the real thing – and yet if we don't attempt to describe Him, how will others know? Even with those close to me, who know me and my experience and preferences well, I sense that I can never fully convey who Jesus is and how and why He's so special. It is not until the Beloved's friends know the lover that they will begin to understand her description of him. So it is with us; as we talk with those who know Jesus, we are warmed by a kindred knowing. I know that you know that I know, etc. The fact that others might not understand should not stop us from sharing, but we need to be aware of the pain of being misunderstood for it often is confused with rejection. We share what seems so simple, pure, perfect and special, and when we are not understood it feels like we are screwed up like a used tissue for it brings pain, confusion, sadness and disappointment.

Let's take the risk though! Faith is believing that God will keep you safe even if everyone else seems to have let you down. Stand with the friends; listen to the Beloved. Use your imagination (however full or poor you consider it to be). Ask the Holy Spirit to enlarge your capacity to see with your spiritual eyes. The Lover is ruddy and radiant – maybe not your idea of the perfect specimen, but capture the breathlessness of her voice and enter as far as you can into the depth of her emotions in this description. What or who is radiant to you? Whatever it is, stretch your imagination then wonder more! God is always lavish. He is always more than we can think or imagine. Walk today in those greater imaginings of who Jesus is revealing Himself to be. You will not be disappointed. Like Isaiah, we would be pretty speechless if we saw seraphs (Isaiah 6:2); the Lover of our soul is more radiant than any seraph. When He comes again with all the hosts of Heaven there will be no doubt which one of the many He is. He is totally outstanding.

Prayer & Contemplation: *Today, remain open-mouthed, wide-eyed and full of wonder! It is this Jesus who looks intimately on you, the precious one of His heart's sacrifice.*

DAY 99

Song of Songs 5:11 (KJV)
His head is as the most fine gold, his locks are bushy, and black as a raven.

Gold is the most coveted of all precious metals, the measure against which a country's credibility and finances are held. 'Purest' means '24 carat'; after refining and refining there are no impurities left. The Lover is refined. His head, the seat of all wisdom, knowledge and choice are underlined in purity; there is nothing more pure. The Beloved sees beyond the surface and into the depth. Her knowledge of him already appears infinite – like a foretaste of John's vision of Jesus in his Revelation.

The Lover is described as having wavy hair. It flows, and there is a sense of 'not a hair out of place' – perfection personified. The hair is black as a raven, one of the larger birds and one of the few birds that is completely black (no grey hairs!)

Perchance the Beloved had watched ravens in her arduous rounds of working her brothers' vineyards and then seen the relationship between the ravens and how the Lover looks and behaves towards her. Certainly the male ruffing his feathers would have created an impression similar, perhaps, to the Lover's wavy hair. The Beloved has certainly observed the Lover well, and each description comes with added bonus – his hair is *not just* wavy, it is as black as a raven's feathers. For the Beloved the initial observation is not enough – it has to be magnified.

Prayer & Contemplation: *Are you generous in your appreciation of those you love and care for? It is so easy to take for granted those people we hold most dear! Even Jesus! Choose to open your mouth today with words of admiration.*

DAY 100

Song of Songs 5:12 (NIV)
His eyes are like doves by the water streams, washed in milk, mounted like jewels.

Echoes return as the Beloved likens the Lover's eyes to doves. He has already described hers thus, and we would do well to ponder all that's been said about the purity and fidelity of doves. Empathy is declared and a deep sense of 'knowing understanding' which is so much more profound than straight knowledge. There are as many mysteries hidden in these words as there are hidden in the soul that lay behind the eyes thus described.

In a typical feminine way the Beloved takes his lead and expands it. The doves are "by a water stream", suggesting life and life-bringing. As their eyes meet so life wells up in the soul of each, but more than that, water is the wherewithal to maintain life and also to encourage it to flourish. As the Beloved brings forth her description you can almost hear her voice tail off into a whisper as her memory refreshes itself on the thought of his eyes. Wonder overrules and she's almost lost in it...

Milk can be a wonderful cleansing agent that will restore lustre to deadened objects. The life in his eyes is clear and bright, sparkling in the light of love. As with any mounted jewel the eye is drawn to the jewel rather than its surround, although without the surround the jewel may lose some of its magnificence. She recognises his eyes are mounted on his face to enhance them, but she is almost oblivious to the detail of his eyelids, brows and lashes.

Prayer & Contemplation: *What does the Beloved's description of the Lover tell you about Jesus? Spend some time to adore Jesus in your own words today. Beyond what He <u>does</u> in your life, choose to adore who He <u>is</u>.*

DAY 101

Song of Songs 5:13 (NIV)
His cheeks are like beds of spice yielding perfume. His lips are like lilies dripping with myrrh.

Spice, perfume, lilies, myrrh! These are so precious and aromatic, delicate yet paradoxically powerful, images of extravagance. Nothing is too good to be used as a description of her Lover. She is almost drunk just on the thoughts of all these things. Lips like lilies! I wonder what sort of lily she has in her mind's eye – certainly not the white, waxen 'death lily' but something sumptuous and inviting. She is imagining herself nuzzled up to his face and drowning in the fragrance.

Prayer & Contemplation:

"Lord, can I risk being so extravagant in my descriptive praise of anyone – even in prayer to You? Could I dare let my imagination run riot and use all the things that are precious to me as descriptions? What if I am not understood; can I risk the rejection and humiliation that would bring? I need to be healed in the area of 'what others will think'. With my head I can say it doesn't matter, but my emotions often tell me otherwise.

"Often I focus on acceptability. If I can't use 'acceptable' descriptions (my perception of acceptability – which is based on what I think others would find acceptable) then I hold back. It is easier to express extravagant praise in written form – but to say something face-to-face seems out of the question! I am haunted by so many sneering, leering, mocking faces and voices that the risk feels huge. But I choose to surrender this area of my life to you too.

"Lord, I choose to begin my praise with You. You is worthy of all adoration and will not misunderstand. But I also choose to praise others, who are made in Your image."

DAY 102

Song of Songs 5:14 (NIV)
His arms are rods of gold set with topaz. His body is like polished ivory decorated with lapis lazuli[19].

The Beloved drops her gaze from the Lover's face to consider his torso. She refers to rods of gold, arms that are firm, strong, straight and bronzed, extolling his power, frame, appearance and preciousness. That could have been enough for most mere mortals but not for the Beloved – there's more! This gold is set with chrysolite. Chrysolite is "the ancient term for the yellow topaz(aluminium fluo-silicate) or yellow quartz."[20]

The word comes from the Greek 'khrosos' meaning 'gold' and 'lithos' meaning 'stone'. Thus the Beloved's added description brings strength to the original. Olivine is 6.5 to 7 in Moh's scale of hardness (the measure by which all rocks are graded), indicating a firmness but also a gentleness. As a rock it could easily be hewn and polished – easily scratched but not likely to break. It's as if she recognises the two qualities in the Lover's arms: his strength in battle and ability to protect her together with his gentleness in love and closeness.

Polished ivory would have been creamy white and gleaming, ivory coming from the tusks of elephants. These days, because of conservation and care for the wild, ivory is no longer used, but in the past it was used for piano keys, cutlery handles, etc.; because of its enduring nature it could take all the handling and wear.

The Beloved's added bonus is 'sapphire' – lapis lazuli. Sapphire is a form of corundum and usually dark blue. With the exception of diamond, which is the only thing that will mark a sapphire, it is one of the hardest minerals known – a precious stone much used in jewellery but also in mechanisms and tools because of its hardness. Corundum is a rather dull stone and it is colourless. Sapphire and ruby are its grander varieties. The colouring for sapphire comes from the fact that there is a trace of titanium in the corundum. Titanium is one of the most precious and coveted metals today. Fine sapphires are

---

[19] Or sapphires
[20] The New Bible Dictionary (p.632); published by IVP (1962); ISBN: 0-85110-820-2

found in the gravels of Ceylon, Siam and Kashmir[21]. For the Beloved to know of such things we begin to appreciate how even in the days of Solomon there was much travel and trade.

If it is lapis lazuli, the colour is still striking (a vivid blue) but this is only a semi-precious stone with weaker properties than sapphire – a pleasing comparison nonetheless.

The Beloved is building up a striking picture of her Lover, her extra descriptions almost being emphasis to her friends as to why he's so much better than others.

Prayer & Contemplation: *The picture of strength, colour, prowess and striking features encourages our imagination to run riot in our endeavours to visualise such a man. We each have a mental image of the Lover in our soul, and probably the image changes to reflect the part of His nature that we are currently experiencing. How do you picture Him? No one person's picture is better or more complete than another's. The mystery of the Lover's soul is a poem which daily brings fresh revelations. The invitation is always to explore further. The choice to explore is always ours.*

---

[21] Sri Lanka, Thailand and Kashmir

DAY 103

Song of Songs 5:15a (NIV)
His legs are pillars of marble set on bases of pure gold.

The Beloved's eyes descend the line of the Lover's torso and arrive at the pillars of strength that maintain him erect but in the blink of an eye carry him swiftly to fight the foe. As we imagine marble pillars that we have seen in churches or other major buildings we become aware of their strength and immovability. They are parts of a building that often remain even when roofs and walls have long since fallen. There is a sense of the eternal in marble pillars.

We sense well-being and security deepen as the Beloved ponders all that these legs mean to her. Like the rest of his body, his legs shine; for marble can be honed and polished like gold and ivory. Light and reflection seem to emanate from every part of him. As he has given himself to the Beloved so she has seen her true reflection in him. No longer is she the darkened-skinned, whimpering slave of her brothers. Now she is *the* Beloved of her Lover. As he stands tall and erect, so she stands similarly alongside him. There is an invincibility about her when she is with him.

Prayer & Contemplation: *Do you feel comfortable being exposed and examined by Jesus? Or are there areas that you have hidden from Him? Will you invite Him to see those hidden areas today and do with them whatever He chooses? You might be surprised at His response!*

DAY 104

Song of Songs 5:15b (NIV)
His appearance is like Lebanon, choice as its cedars.

Because Lebanon has been a country in my generation, I have always read any reference to the word Lebanon as referring to that country. This just goes to show how a knowledge of Bible lands, times, and culture are important in order to understand what's being said in the Word! For only in modern times has Lebanon been anything other than a mountain range!

The word Lebanon comes from Hebrew and means 'white' or 'snowy'.

> *It is a mountain range commencing near Tyre (on the Mediterranean coast) and it runs North-eastward through Syria nearly parallel to the sea coast sometimes as high as 9000 feet above the sea.*[22]

> *Another traditional symbol, the famed cedars of Lebanon were prized for their natural beauty and their exceptional durability as building materials.*[23]

Solomon built the Temple and nearby royal apartments and...

> *...these large public buildings: the House of the forest of Lebanon, the House of pillars and the Hall of the Throne...*[24]

Is the Beloved describing the Lover as the mountain range or a splendid building? It could be either, or more likely both, for in her eyes nothing manmade nor anything created can hold a torch to her Lover.

The more I walk with Jesus the more light shines through Him as through a diamond, and each new ray brings fresh insight into who He is. The unfathomable dimension of His character fills me with awe such that I feel I can explore no further, and also fills me with hope which brings an invitation and expectation of discovering more.

---

[22] Young's Analytical Concordance
[23] Atlas of the Bible, p22. Used by permission of The Reader's Digest Association, Inc.
[24] Atlas of the Bible, p102. Used by permission of The Reader's Digest Association, Inc.

The Lover's appearance is "choice in its cedars" – not just any old cedar which would have been fairly special but the *choicest* of cedars – the strongest, the straightest, with the most perfume. Superlatives are the norm falling from the Beloved's lips. Love always accentuates the positive.

As my own daughter is in love, sighs and daydreams are the order of the day in our household. He can do no wrong and be no wrong, and yet there is still this yearning for more. To watch before my own eyes as love accentuates the positive and grows the spirit is a delight. It reinvigorates my own love, restores good memories and rehearses all the reasons why I married the man I did. "My first love is a blazing fire. I feel His powerful love in me."[25] If only first love would not become sullied by the cares, concerns and crises of this fallen world!

Prayer & Contemplation: *How was your first love for Jesus? Has it become choked by the cares of life? If so, ask forgiveness for the things you have allowed to distract you from simply enjoying being with Him. Choose to make space for resting with your Lover and spending quality time together.*

---

[25] 'My first love is a blazing fire' by Stuart Townend; SOF page 930;
© 1996 Kingsway/Thankyou music.

DAY 105

Song of Songs 5:16a (NIV)
His mouth is sweetness itself; he is altogether lovely.

Did she forget his mouth on her way down? No, for she mentions his lips. It's as if this particular part of him is very special to her and needs a repeat mention. To know sweetness is to have tasted it, and we are left in little doubt that kisses have passed between his lips and hers. However, I read into this something deeper. Out of the mouth of the Lover have come words of love, affirmation and uplift. Here is someone mirroring to her parts of her that she didn't believe had ever existed. His soul has spoken through his mouth and brought life to her. She has exalted him and his physical appearance as much as she can, but there are few words to describe his soul. She has never met another's soul before, and neither has she met her own. It is no small wonder, therefore, that she is limited to "he is altogether lovely"! These words bring his worth out – not physical appearance, skills or prowess but *who he is*. How these words are uttered is probably more significant than the words themselves. She has reached the point of describing the indescribable – a point of awed stillness, a silence between friends that is precious beyond belief, a knowing of souls that brings a taste of eternity to earth.

Prayer & Contemplation: *Do you experience Jesus as "altogether lovely"? If not, what description comes to mind? Is it one that is birthed out of religious expectations or one birthed out of a freeing relationship? Jesus sees you as "altogether lovely" too. How do you perceive yourself as a new creation? How does that affect your ability to approach your Lover? Thank Jesus for His cleansing work on the cross, which enables you to both enjoy one another's loveliness without expectation, guilt or demands.*

DAY 106

Song of Songs 5:16b
This is my beloved, this is my friend, daughters of Jerusalem.

Light dawns for the Beloved as she walks into the hushed whispers of love. There is a relationship here that is a gift – not a legally binding agreement but a freely given gift. For the first time the Beloved describes her Lover as her *friend*. Those who subdivide the scriptures have chosen to call the companions of the Beloved 'friends' but she does not call them such. She addresses them as 'daughters of Jerusalem'. Her Lover she calls friend.

What is a friend? A parent is one who chooses to bring a child into the world and therefore should have moral obligations to that child as both child and adult. A child is brought into the world by a parent and therefore has a relationship with them that is no choice of its own. A husband and wife have (in our western culture) a choice in whom they marry, but once married there is a legal requirement to love each other, to care for and support one another. A slave or servant or employee has a contractual agreement to serve the master. The master/boss has a contractual or ethical responsibility towards their slaves/workers. A friend is one who chooses to give for no other reason than love. A friend does not have to care, provide, seek the good of another; it is a sacrificial choice that has no binding agreements attached. Friends may make agreements (as with David and Jonathan) but there is no obligation or compulsion.

Jesus is often called 'friend of sinners'. There is no compulsion for Him to be so, but it is His choice! Jesus chose time and again the lost, forsaken, hurting people of this world to befriend. We see it all through the Gospels. He hasn't stopped! Jesus Christ, Son of the Living God, Lord, King, Saviour, Shepherd, Redeemer has chosen to be both my Lover and my Friend. My mouth, my mind, my heart and my soul fall open in awe and wonder. Like the Beloved I am stilled and silenced by such a lavish gift and profound relationship!

Prayer & Contemplation: *Who are the friends who have chosen to stand by your side, no matter what? Thank God for these friends today, and also for the most faithful friend of all – Jesus.*

DAY 107

Song of Songs 5:16b
This is my beloved, this is my friend, daughters of Jerusalem.

The Beloved comes to a place where she has not only a Lover but a Friend. This is 'no strings attached' vulnerability!

Friendship opens love up to the potential for betrayal; only a friend can get close enough to betray. Betrayal is so painful it becomes deadly. Those who have been betrayed know only too well how it destroys the soul and incarcerates it in a place 'never to be hurt like that again'. The twist is that in making such a vow we also close ourselves up to ever really being known and loved again. Unconditional love asks us to take the risk of betrayal for the promise of certain hope, worth, security and love. How the Beloved has grown as we've journeyed through her story with her! Perhaps this statement, more than any other, reveals who she is, where she is and where her hope lies. She has taken the risk to be vulnerable; she has risked humiliation and rejection from the daughters of Jerusalem and, having been beaten and having let her Lover leave her, she now vulnerably declares where her longings lie: with her Lover and her Friend. Looking back to 5:1, the 'friends' have recognised the specialness of the relationship that the two of them have, for they call them both friends and lovers. Often it takes other people to spell out for us what we appear blind to see! What it is to have those around us who are for us and whose opinions and views we trust! This doesn't mean that we should follow blindly, because we are responsible for our own choice. However, true friendship makes sacrifices for the good of the other.

Here we pause to recognise the gift given by the daughters of Jerusalem. In recognising the friendship that now exists between the Lover and the Beloved they give the gift of their friendship away. The relationship that the friends have with the Beloved will never be the same again. They will have lost something obviously precious to them, but it is a gift freely given for the greater good of both the Lover and the Beloved. Friendship can never be held in a clenched fist or even in a cupped hand – to have the potential for life and growth it must be held in a completely open hand. My experience suggests, though, that however painful the grief of losing 'what has been' may be, the joy of 'what will be' will far outweigh it. So often, what we choose to freely give away God multiplies back to us a hundredfold. The journey for the friends will be as exciting as it will be for the lovers.

Through the deep pain of 'having blown it' in her own attitudes, the deep pain of physical and emotional pain and humiliation, and even the potential pain of rejection and betrayal of her friends, the Beloved comes to a place of the simplicity of her longings: to be known and to be acceptable. Friendship is such a key word. It asks us the biggest question of all: to whom will you give yourself unequivocally?

Prayer & Contemplation:

"Lord, the path of choice is wide. Having decided to give ourselves to You, we find that that this choice is not a single track – 'Don't step off the edge!' – but a vast panoply of options that all should include You."[26]

---

[26] Though the gate and path are narrow (Matthew 7:14) we have to choose the right path from all the options offered to us: be a quiet Christian, noisy Christian, 'just follow' Christian, or be a Beloved of the Lord.

DAY 108

Song of Songs 6:1 (NASB)
Where has your beloved gone, O most beautiful among women?
Where has your beloved turned, that we may seek him with you?

These questions bring offers of assistance. They affirm who the Beloved is and what the relationship is between speakers and the one spoken to! They are all still friends. She is still held in high esteem. Friendship has come through, the victor! These questions reveal the anxiety to help her in her distress – typical questions when panic sets in.

Often in a situation of panic we ask the first thing that comes into our minds, and therefore it is not reasoned out. The Beloved has already recounted that she didn't get the door open in time to see the Lover, so how will she know which way he went?! How rightly we often describe it as 'blind panic'! It descends on us with a blinkered grip, and everything seems to fly away.

Sometimes by not thinking, by going straight in, a little peace is brought to calm the anxiety of another, which enables them to think clearly and to realise that they do have more facts at their disposal than they at first recognised. The friends' offer of help in the search will have brought comfort and reassurance to the Beloved, especially in the light of the fact that all previous requests for help brought a beating! The enormity of the task is now shared, and suddenly it seems much less impossible. Using words she has heard before they bring her to the calmer place of reassurance. The sorrow and grief she now feels has a productive outlet by which to make its escape. The ups and downs of life are much more easily put into perspective when we have the encouragement of the presence of others, particularly 'safe' others.

Reason and calm prevail as the Beloved realises where the Lover will be. Hear her sighs and the anticipation in her next words...

Prayer & Contemplation: *Can you identify someone who is currently acting like the Beloved – responding to her challenging circumstances in an emotional flurry? Instead of avoiding them, ask the Father to help you be a true friend. Offer encouragement, and share their pain.*

DAY 109

Song of Songs 6:2 (NASB)
My beloved has gone down to his garden, to the beds of balsam, to pasture his flock in the gardens and gather lilies.

She recalls his words, probably hearing his voice in her mind. She realises the truth in what he has said to her and she knows – not just as facts in her mind but with that deep reassurance of soul and spirit that defies description. A confidence flows back into her, and her head, which has dropped to ground level, rises with the message of hope he has sown deep within! He will be in his best place, his favourite place. He will be waiting for her there. How foolish she was to have panicked and forgotten! How quickly adverse circumstances cause both her and us to forget the foundation of truth we stand upon! If he was hurting because of her apparent rejection of him then it was more than likely he'd go somewhere to sort himself out – and where better than a quiet, familiar place?

We can learn much from both of them: not to jump to conclusions; not to listen to the voice of past experiences and project them onto others; to listen to the voice of truth; to know and be known so that we can come to a reasoned place in time of panic; to have those around us who will support and point us in the right direction.

The godhead is three persons, and they work together. We need others; we cannot function completely alone. Look at the beautiful things that the Lover used to describe the Beloved and bring life to her soul. The balance between reason and soul desires is fine; how encouraged and growing we are when we hold that tension, neither moving too far toward reason nor toward soul desire.

Prayer & Contemplation: *Do you face challenging circumstances in your life right now? Take a moment to recall times when God has helped you in the past. Remembering the miracles and victories of old can help you find peace and faith for the present.*

DAY 110

Song of Songs 6:3 (NIV)
I am my beloved's and my beloved is mine; he browses among the lilies.

I think I could ponder a lifetime on "I am my Beloved's" and not get to the bottom of it, to say nothing of the rest of the verse. It expresses an all-inclusive belonging! This is not possessiveness, for that would be exclusive and shut out everyone else. This is one of the great mysteries of faith: that my Lover is mine but also yours and millions of others'. From my place of 'mine' I share and touch your place of 'mine', and in the touching both our understandings are deepened. For in sharing my 'mine' I also share all the 'mine's that others have already shared with me, and in reaching your 'mine' all of us touch you, and all those 'mine's who have touched you, touch me!

Even if I do not speak about the intimacy of 'mine' you will still share my 'mine' just by me being me. When I choose to own and speak out of my 'mine', my 'being' is owned and, more importantly, the gift is owned. So this 'mine' I share is a love-gift from me to you, and it is magnified and multiplied by Jesus through countless other 'mine's who have gifted themself to me.

It seems that the wonder of belonging so completely is so profound that I only grasp it fleetingly before it is swamped by demands and even disbelief. The world seems to perpetually try to discredit and destroy the wonder of this love, and it becomes a moment by moment battle not to lose sight of its depth. The Beloved has found this already – doubt and failure have already sown their seeds in the newly tilled soil of her soul. I identify with that; it seems no sooner is there a fresh touch from the Lover of my life than everything conspires against it to undermine and suck me away. It seems unfair, but it is a result of my fallenness? It does however keep me thirsty, keep me looking, keep me willing to face the struggle to change.

I am a browser. I love to browse through bookshops, in particular. It can be a very expensive occupation as temptation is regularly on my shoulder. But I love to browse as I walk. Creation speaks volumes to me and it is not difficult to imagine the Lover browsing among the lilies – we've already examined the fact that the Lover likens the Beloved to the fairest lily of all. A browser scans much but usually stops and gives in depth perusal to something particularly eye-catching. As we shall see, this is what happens to the Lover.

Prayer & Contemplation: *Choose to stop and simply browse today. Take into your spirit the detail of who Jesus is. Adore Him and admire Him. Then take that with you, into the day, to share with others. Also, keep your spiritual eyes open throughout the day to see what you can learn about your Lover from other people.*

DAY 111

Song of Songs 6:4 (NLT)
You are beautiful, my darling, like the lovely city of Tirzah. Yes, as beautiful as Jerusalem, as majestic as an army with billowing banners.

Suddenly the Lover is back. Is this in the flesh? In her memory? As an allegory it can be left to our imaginations. As the Beloved ceases from her panic and drops into the stillness of her newfound soul and her ownership of feelings, she discovers he is not gone, neither is all the truth he has spoken to her which has led to the revelation of the beauty of her soul.

His words are back with her, caressing and soothing her in her anxiety. The world, through the watchmen, has tried in vain to destroy who she is. The truth, through the Lover's words, restores and even brings fresh life to her. I remind myself that I am called to be a restorer of streets with dwellings, and find myself challenged by the words and deeds I employ that destroy rather than restore. There is potential here to enter into personal self-contempt, to inwardly beat myself up. But, like the Beloved, I choose to walk into the truth of who I am in God, to kneel before the cross and seek the forgiveness of my Lover. I have fallen, but in His truth and with His victory I do not remain so. I rise from confession with a new determination to live as I was designed, not as I have become ensnared.

Jerusalem I know, but where, what or who is Tirzah? Tirzah means 'delight' in Hebrew. The biblical references are sometimes to a person: the youngest daughter of Zelophahad, mentioned in the books of Numbers and Joshua. Other references are to a place: a city in Ephraim or Manasseh mentioned in Joshua, 1 Kings and 2 Kings. Tersa is three hours east of Samaria, whilst Taluza is six miles northeast of Nablus. Here the reference it is more likely to be a town than the daughter.

Jerusalem means 'possession of peace' – a city with one of the most chequered histories of ownership. It was originally counted to Benjamin, and it was built on four hills: Zion, Acra, Mariah and Besetha.

We take on board the magnificence and bounty that is being described here. For her Lover, such abundance is overwhelming. Imagine an army with banners trooping in the sunlight, armour and weaponry gleaming! It is almost enough to blind the opposition into capitulation before a sword is lifted in anger!

Catch the irony of one recently beaten, almost bowed down with shame and humiliation, being described in this opening burst as "majestic". From 5:7 when she is in total despair, through the encouragement of her friends and her remembrance of him, to the place of serene majesty. How love and affirmation restores life! It is like nothing else. At receiving such praise we might have thought she would want to flee because of all that's happened. Not so... As we will see, it is the Lover who cannot cope with the sight...

Prayer & Contemplation: *Does self-contempt keep you held back in life from being whom God intended? Do you see yourself through the lens of your sin or through the lens of the Father's forgiveness? Confess your sins to Him today, and then choose to live as you were designed, through the victory of the Cross of Christ.*

DAY 112

Song of Songs 6:5-7 (NLT)

Turn your eyes away, for they overpower me. Your hair falls in waves, like a flock of goats winding down the slopes of Gilead. Your teeth are as white as sheep that are freshly washed. Your smile is flawless, each tooth matched with its twin. Your cheeks are like rosy pomegranates behind your veil.

The Lover is overcome and is unable to grasp all his eyes see. Overwhelmed by the view of her soul he asks her to avert her gaze. What were her eyes saying to him? Could he see even further into her soul than he could at the first encounter? The richness of her soul is impossible for this eloquent, majestic Lover to absorb. "Too much!" he cries, and he drops his eyes to other parts of her which feel safer to him and repeats his previous description of her. Lost for words in one of those 'knowing' moments, he falls back on the familiar.

When describing the Beloved, the Lover uses identical words to 4:1-3 except this time round some parts are omitted. Is he forgetful? No, just totally overcome... breathless, speechless and totally besotted.

Prayer & Contemplation: *Jesus is overcome with love for His Bride. Do you have the same affection for the Church? For the Christian believers in your neighbourhood? Ask Him to help you to see them through His eyes and with His lavish love.*

DAY 113

Song of Songs 6:8-9 (NIV)

Sixty queens there may be, and eighty concubines, and virgins beyond number; but my dove, my perfect one, is unique, the only daughter of her mother, the favourite of the one who bore her. The young women saw her and called her blessed; the queens and concubines praised her.

What is the significance of the numbers sixty and eighty? Is it a case of 'pick the first number that comes into your head and keep on increasing it' as an emphatic means of demonstrating the beauty of his Beloved? Or are those figures a reality – does he have sixty wives he is officially married to and eighty to whom he isn't? Whichever, we can't escape the fact that he is totally besotted with the Beloved. She is the one and only. There is none like her.

"Unique" – how hard that word is for us to come to terms with personally. The overwhelming drive in the world is conformity and uniformity. The overwhelming drive in us is to belong – and if belonging means burying our uniqueness then so be it. Watch a group of teenagers rebel against the constraints of school uniform and then see those same teenagers go out together later in the day all wearing the same colour or style or label. Our God-given longing to be uniquely who we were created to be struggles against the God-given desire to belong. It is a sign of our rebellion and fall.

We shut God out of our soul, try to be God ourselves and are doomed to fail in the fulfilment of our basic inner desires for acceptance and significance. Why? Because the world cannot give us either. It lures us all alone into its snare – deeper and deeper into the futility of our unmet longings. Only in God can these be fulfilled. Only in eternity will they be entirely satisfied. In this life, as we begin to walk into the uniqueness of who we are and dare to risk believing that we are acceptable and significant to God, will we find the fulfilment of being acceptable and significant in the here and now.

It is our very uniqueness that draws us to one and repels us from another. Often it is that same uniqueness that was so attractive which also becomes the wedge between us. We struggle so much with being unique because it means we are always set apart, always different. The seemingly inbuilt drive in us, though, is to be the same. The church on the one hand understands this separateness, this being called apart and different, *but* in our separateness this desire for conformity within separation becomes destructive. In this age of instant communication and knowledge it is too easy to go looking for places and people with whom we have the most similarities. Rather than learn to live in unity, we hear instead, "Be uniform," and we rebel or are repelled for we don't or won't fit.

To prove ourselves acceptable we actively, if unconsciously, kill off our uniqueness and in the choice destroy that part of the image of God for which we carry the imprint. No one of us can completely be the image of God for if we could then we would *be* God – but if we stifle the unique image of God that resides in us that part of Him will not be discovered or added to the whole.

The Beloved – so unique in the Lover's eyes – is probably thought of by others as one of many – and certainly by her family she is considered of little value.

In all his words, the Lover is exhorting the Beloved to be her unique self, to display her image of God to all who will choose to behold; but this is an infinitely risky path littered with the storms of words, actions and perceptions that trip us up, even causing us to stumble to soul-death. How we need to understand that there is no thing, no word, no one that can separate us from the love of God! The Image-giver has his total concentration, effort and love pouring in the direction of the image-bearer. His greatest desire is that we worship Him and through our worship (in all its forms) display His image to this longing world, so that they too may be released to be the image-bearers they were created to be.

Prayer & Contemplation: Do you strive to be similar to others, in order to be accepted, or are you willing to be the unique individual God has created you to be? Note that it is the Beloved's uniqueness that draws the Lover to her, not her conformity.

DAY 114

Song of Songs 6:9b (NIV)
...the only daughter of her mother, the favorite of the one who bore her. The young women saw her and called her blessed; the queens and concubines praised her.

The Lover is still struggling to find the pinnacle of praise to bestow on the Beloved. In his ascent we find out two facts about the Beloved, not yet revealed, which help to bring some more understanding of the state we find her in at the beginning of the story. She is the only daughter of her mother, which when one considers the value placed on women and daughters may explain why she is tending all the others' vineyards. Brother would not choose or deign to serve brother, but sister would be expected to be at brother's beck and call. She could, of course, be the only child of her mother, and in fact her brothers would be her half-brothers for it would not be impossible for her father to have more than one wife – another reason for the bitterness she holds in her heart towards her brothers and perhaps an explanation as to why neither father nor mother stepped in to stop the abuse.

However, if the brothers were natural brothers, the next statement adds further explanation to why she was mistreated: the Beloved was Mum's favourite. Already in Scripture we have seen the bitterness and resentment in families where one child is preferred over another: Joseph and his brothers. We saw there how God purposed good out of Joseph's painful circumstances and his brothers' evil intent. Here too we find that even through this deep dark pain of abuse God is breaking in with eternal purpose and intense love. Somehow, when we've been deprived of love and protection from the places we should have received it, when we receive God's love there is such a release that we can't wait to talk about it, but neither can we wait to experience Him again – and so we are drawn into the eternal thirst for love.

Everyone who saw the Beloved, after the Lover had brought about such deep internal transformation in her, couldn't help but remark at the feast that was now before their eyes. Even the Lover had noticed, in his besotted state, that everyone else was wide-eyed at the power of love. Like water transforms a dying wilting plant into a lush, vibrant and fruitful one, so love transforms a dead and dying soul so that no-one can fail to miss its mark. They may not understand the whys and wherefores, but they will take notice.

Prayer & Contemplation: *Do you perceive yourself to be socially disadvantaged? In what way? Just as God turned around the circumstances of Joseph and the Beloved for good, so He desires to do it in your life. It will not only bring blessing to you but also to many others. Thank Him for His perfect plan, and ask Him to help you accept the way He has created you.*

DAY 115

Song of Songs 6:10
<u>Friends</u> *Who is this that appears like the dawn, fair as the moon, bright as the sun, majestic as the stars in procession?*

Having been asked to help in the search, having asked all the whys and wherefores of the Lover, the friends join in the Lover's eulogy of the Beloved.

What is it about the dawn that draws poets, writers and lyricists to use its special charms? They say the night is darkest just before the dawn. If so then the arrival of the dawn must bring the first glimmer of light and hope. All-pervading darkness seeps into every crack and emotion with a sense of foreboding and finality, whereas the dawn brings all the fresh hope of the new day as yet unlived and unfulfilled. In the darkness we are tempted to remember all the dull, mundane, bad, wrong and evil things. Light arrives and suddenly the intensity of the nasty things of life fades. Jesus does that for us when He brings His light into our darkness. The weight of our burdens, cares and worries seems lighter and our step freer.

All the natural light-bringers across the universe link together to bring hope into this scenario – the light-providers (sun and stars) as well as the light-reflector (the moon). In Heaven we will have no need of them for God will be the light, but until then His eternal presence is symbolised by the created light.

To the friends and the Lover everything about the Beloved is so full of hope there is no temptation to fear, doubt or shame. Fair, bright and majestic, she moves into their lives with such promise of contentment.

Prayer & Contemplation: *Do you feel that you are experiencing a dark night in your life? Do you find it hard to see clearly what God's purposes are? Do you feel oppressed and lonely? As surely as the sun rises in the morning, a new day is purposed for your life too.*

DAY 116

Song of Songs 6:11 (NASB)
I went down to the orchard of nut trees to see the blossoms of the valley, to see whether the vine had budded or the pomegranates had bloomed.

The Lover has been as full of longing as the Beloved. Had he gone away in desire rather than in disgust when there was no answer at the Beloved's door? Is this the report of where he had disappeared to during her frantic and fearful search? Or was it where had been at the point before he'd gone to find her? Either is a possibility, and in some ways it matters not which of the two it was. The significance of his words lies far more in the hope, potential and promise he is seeking.

There is something comforting and secure about a grove of nut trees in a valley. It conjures up romance. Lazy days, wandering arm in arm 'twixt the shadow and the light, enjoying the fragrance of the woods and the elixir of love. The hope of fruitfulness is behind every one of his words. Feasting is on his agenda – feasting to overflow in every sense. You can almost feel his imagination running riot and stirring his loins. His words echo the longings and words of the Beloved in verses two and three. His wish, the fruitfulness demanded by the manly soul, and hers, with the beauty expected of the female soul – different but the same, each indicating the intense desire felt for the other.

It behoves us well to find understanding in our communication of love. For if we don't understand that each individual may give and receive love in a different way then we may miss or reject the love given and the rejection will take its grip on both parties, driving a wedge between them. How imperative it is that we not only talk about what is important to us but that we communicate why. This imperative is superseded only by the need to listen – really listen – and understand what we are being told. Here is where love so often falls to pieces, never to be put back together again.

Prayer & Contemplation: *There is an expectation on the part of Jesus that we, His Bride, will be fruitful. But it is not an onerous, demanding expectation. It is an expectation that out of love and* *relationship with Him fruitfulness will happen. As part of the vine, it is up to the vine and its resources to bring fruitfulness. A branch cannot be fruitful on its own... although we try to! Neither is the fruit borne for the good of the branch. No, the fruit is for those who will come and pick it, the branch having no say whatsoever as to who that may be. It is the same with the nuts on the nut trees and the pomegranates on theirs.*

DAY 117

Song of Songs 6:12
Before I realised it my desire set me [among the royal chariots of my people / among the chariots of Amminadab / among the chariots of the people of the prince].

This is a difficult verse to understand for someone who is neither male nor Middle-eastern. I suspect that the strength of the Lover's desire is so powerful that it is similar to when he leads out his chariots in procession or battle. He is clearly not physically removed as he continues his narrative half a verse later – but mentally he could be whisked away, imagining all the pomp and exhilaration.

I suggest that these words are the Lover's pinnacle of describing how he feels: the sense of belonging, fulfilment and purpose that confers to him the tightness of it all.

Such is the intensity of Jesus' love for us – corporately and individually. Are we saved? Yes! But also *being* saved! How this should present a challenge to us, to so walk in the love of Jesus that we can't help but love! Should we love the lovely? Yes! But we should also love the unlovely!

Prayer & Contemplation: *Ask God to increase the flow of His love in your life – especially towards the unlovely and disregarded. Ask Him to open your eyes to those whom He would desire you to express His grace and kindness towards.*

DAY 118

Song of Songs 6:13a (NASB)
Come back, come back, O Shulammite; Come back, come back, that we may gaze at you!

A Shulammite is a female inhabitant of either Shulem or Shunem in Issachar. This is the only verse of Scripture that uses the word, and so there is little to determine which of the two places it may have been. Shunem means 'uneven' and is a city near Chesulloth, on a steep slope of Gilboa. It is now called Salem or Sulim. In 1 Kings 1; 2 and 2 Kings 4 we hear of the inhabitants of Shunem being called Shunammites. We are left in some confusion as to with what or whom the comparison is being made.

Without a shadow of a doubt the friends are referring to the Beloved! She seems to have disappeared again! Is this physically, or has she just retreated behind her veil or her old shame? Is she present in body but hiding her soul? 'The lights are on but no-one's at home'? We already know that the friends have begun to recognise things in her that they've never seen before. This underlines the deep and wholly attractive beauty that they've found in her soul. When it is not there they miss it!

When the beauty of who we are is revealed only in brief glimpses, then others miss us too! Perhaps not many are afforded that rare privilege of entering our soul, but once they have tasted the fruit of who we are, subsequent encounters are expectant of more. When we choose, for whatever reason, to hide, then we withhold the fruit of the vine from those who are hungry.

The friends want to gaze on the Beloved – not just to feast on her outer beauty but to drink from the deep wells of who she is. A gaze is not something fleeting, but it is long and lingering. It may be feasting for the gazer, but it can feel like devouring for the one being gazed upon... until of course those who gaze are prepared, from the security of your soul, to open the shelters of their own soul and grant reciprocal gazing.

Prayer & Contemplation: *Do you hide your fruit from those around? Choose to open your heart today. Ask the Spirit to help you in this.*

DAY 119

Song of Songs 6:13b (NIV)
Why would you gaze on the Shulammite as on the dance of Mahanaim?

A rhetorical question? A thought voiced out loud? Can he see her in reality? Or only in his memory? Are the verses that follow his question the answer to the question posed? What is the dance of Mahanaim? Does this provide a clue to why the question is posed?

Much confusion reigns amongst translators and commentators alike. There is debate over the division of chapters and over who says what and why. But two thoughts strike me as I've read other translations and a commentary:

1. Mahanaim was a place of sanctuary set up by Joshua. Linking this thought with the Beloved's chequered history would identify the Lover and being with him as a place of sanctuary and release from her oppression – just as Jesus declared that he had come to bring release for the oppressed.[27] We too can be released from what others have wanted us to be. We can receive the freedom that Jesus declared He would bring as we enter into knowledge of Him.

2. There is a sense of victory here. Some translators render this verse as speaking of a victory celebration between two armies. This continues to underline for me the victory won by the Lover for the Beloved as he and his words have brought (and bought) her out of her slavery. There is every reason why both the Beloved and her friends should want to dance and celebrate. This is victory over what has so far been lifelong enslavement. In the victory celebration the Lover catches fresh vision of the Beloved, and as we move into chapter 7, we shall join with him in feasting his eyes on this fresh revelation of who the Beloved is, as she enters more fully into this new life of being true to herself.

Prayer & Contemplation: Do you need to be released from others' expectations? Claim the freedom that Jesus has won for you through the Cross. State your freedom out loud as an act of faith.

---

[27] Luke 4:18

DAY 120

Song of Songs 7:1 (NIV)
How beautiful your sandaled feet, O prince's daughter! Your graceful legs are like jewels, the work of an artist's hands.

It seems to me as if the Lover has taken a leaf out of the Beloved's book; no longer are his statements of adoration just simple 'one-liners' but they are extended by additional information. In her friends it seems that he found freedom too, a greater freedom to express himself. He is even more poetic than he thought himself to be. This is a risky business – for such an important man to be making such public declaration! Can you imagine the tabloid headlines of today if such a public figure was heard to be so eloquently and emphatically besotted? He would be hung out to dry by public ridicule – totally belittled! I don't suppose the risk was any less there; there was probably an ancient version of a tabloid even then! However, love wins over the potential for shame, and so we have recorded for us some of the most powerful, evocative, sensual and erotic narrative found anywhere; tantalising enough to arouse a response in the reader but not titillating nor crude to denigrate either participants or readers.

Starting at the point of dance, he begins with her feet. They are sandalled! She is no longer a barefoot slave. Already, even at her feet, her past is behind her, and she has moved beyond enslavement and into respectability and honour.

Has her birthright really changed? Is she really a prince's daughter? I think not, but in his eyes she has every reason to be considered thus!

He doesn't just say, "Your legs are like jewels," but he is studying their movement and describes them as graceful. Any awkwardness of the slave or gawkiness of the teenager has long since gone, and she moves with the alluring grace of being the prince's daughter. Deportment extraordinaire! Who would have thought that not long since these legs had been trudging vineyards to tend the vines and climbing mountains to feed the flocks? Her legs should have been muscular, and now they are relaxed and graceful.

"Like jewels" – has he gone back to his former descriptive ways? Not a bit of it! For these are not just any old jewels; these are the finest – handcrafted by master workmen! They are not haphazardly formed but fashioned with every potential for grace and lithe movement.

Let's just pause for a moment, disturb the flow of beauty personified and remind ourselves that in allegory form this is Christ describing us: you and me, male and female, individually and corporately.

Genesis 1:27,31
So God created man in his own image, in the image of God he created him; male and female he created them… God saw all that he had made, and it was very good.

It is often said, "God doesn't create rubbish." We are image-bearers, and we have the choice to live revealing that image or hiding that image – to be true to the image or to bear a false image. As God formed and fashioned us in our mother's wombs, so His were craftsman's hands that fashioned our graceful legs. When we put ourselves down either in word or thought, we are rebelling – we're telling God and others that He got it wrong.

Prayer & Contemplation: *Catch your breath in wonder, and dare to receive these words as personal – from Jesus to you – into the core of your being. Whatever lies you have been fed (even by yourself) over the years, make the conscious choice to allow these words to move beyond your mind and into your heart and soul. Dare to believe the truth, lay aside the baggage and listen to your Creator!*

DAY 121

Song of Songs 7:2-3 (NIV)
Your navel is a rounded goblet that never lacks blended wine. Your waist is a mound of wheat encircled by lilies. Your breasts are like two fawns, like twin fawns of a gazelle.

We return to the Lover as his eyes course up the Beloved's torso. It is left to our imagination and sense of decency as to how much more of her is physically revealed at this moment of time, but he has certainly had opportunity for close study of her form. A rounded goblet suggests the regal – not just any drinking container but a *goblet*, one designed to hold intoxicating beverage. Again only the best will do: blended wine and unending quantities of it. To make blended wine you must have access to several vineyards and varieties of grape, plus other orchards to bring the other flavours of fruit to bear. In my mind's ear I hear Oz Clarke and Jilly Goolden of BBC's 'Food and Drink' programme waxing lyrical about all the things they can smell and taste in wine. The Lover's palate is fine-tuned and can taste the blend and know the effort that has gone into producing this fine wine. I wonder if the experts have tasted such a profound vintage. 'Only the finest' is what the Beloved gives to him.

The excess continues with mounds of wheat encircled by lilies. From beverage to quench his thirst and stir his passions there is food to feed him and beautiful, full flowers to feast his eyes upon. From a distance he is admiring her; with all his senses he is close by devouring her.

Can Christ feel this intensity for me? Yes and more, for we are limited by human language and passion. There will come a time when we will enter the eternal divine with no end to passion. I sometimes catch myself inwardly pondering, "Won't it be boring to do nothing but passion, God?" From the limitations of the human it might appear so, but with the merest snatched glimpses of the eternal, the potential is awesome!

There is no new description of her breasts, just a pondering again of the youthful softness and playfulness – an alluring and beguiling difference between his anatomy and hers. His chest is described by her as strong and armour-plated, hers as soft, gentle and innocent.

For both there is security and a promise of protective fulfilment: shelter, comfort and nurturing.

Prayer & Contemplation: *We live in this fallen world only for a short season. When we reach our heavenly home, we will experience the fullness of God's passion and enjoy rest in His presence – forever! Pray for endurance and faithfulness to 'run the race' here on Earth. There then awaits a great reward in the life to come.*

DAY 122

Song of Songs 7:4 (KJV)
Thy neck is as a tower of ivory; thine eyes like the fishpools in Heshbon, by the gate of Bathrabbim: thy nose is as the tower of Lebanon which looketh toward Damascus.

Was David's tower an ivory tower? Ivory comes from elephant's tusks and is able to be highly polished and intricately carved – strong and hardwearing. The 'ivory tower' is beguiling as the Lover draws ever closer to that which gives him entry to her soul...

Her eyes are not just pools but *the* pools. Heshbon means 'stronghold' and is the name of a rebellious city of Reuben and Gad. It first belonged to Moab and then to Ammon. It's situated 20 miles east of Jordan on the north end of the Dead Sea. Bath Rabbin means 'daughter of many' and is a gate of the city of Hebron near which were two pools. By likening the Beloved's eyes to these pools, is the Lover purely being poetic, with all the watery and reflective parallels that can be drawn? Or was he seeing further and recognising the promise and potential he saw in her soul: the strength of character that had withstood so much and enabled her to do more than just survive but come out of it whole and strong?

Is there promise here for us too? As Jesus looks into our 'pools' does He see and inspire hope that we too can be restored to the creation that we were intended to be? I think so for experience tells me that the longer we gaze into the soul of the One who so completely loves us, the more we will find ourselves transformed by all that we see in His Soul.

We've already noted that Lebanon is a mountain range and not a country. Damascus is an ancient city, already established in the days when this was written and still in existence today; a major city, rich, prosperous and powerful, the centre of much of the life of the area.

The Beloved's nose, described like the mountain, is obviously a feature of her face.

Prayer & Contemplation: *God sees you as a 'new creation', filled with His potential for love and spiritual fruit. Choose to speak out the truth of who you are in Jesus – in prayer and with other people.*

DAY 123

Song of Songs 7:5 (NIV)
Your head crowns you like Mount Carmel. Your hair is like royal tapestry; the king is held captive by its tresses.

Into my mind comes the story of Elijah and the prophets of Baal on Mount Carmel, where the awesome power of God is displayed as totally superior to other gods'.[28] But I suspect that the Lover is referring here to the sight of Mount Carmel from a distance. How it would stand out on the horizon, a mountain among mountains, proud, dominant and resplendent. Just as Mount Carmel draws the eye from amongst the other mountains, so does her head amongst other heads or from the rest of her bodily features; however resplendent they are, nothing surpasses her head.

Her hair is like a royal tapestry, the finest of threads on the finest of canvas, weaving the finest of designs, created by the finest of workmen. Rich in colour and texture, nothing would surpass a tapestry in the palace. Is it any wonder that the King is attracted to the richness of her flowing hair? Dark and falling alluringly across her shoulders, the Lover is overwhelmed and transfixed. Nothing could tear him away from all that is in front of him. The promise of more waits impatiently to be possessed.

Prayer & Contemplation: *The miracle of uniqueness is that each one of us 'stands out' to God. We do not blend into the crowd; he <u>notices</u> us, individually. Be confident today and keep your head raised! If God is for us, who can be against us?*

---

[28] 1 Kings 18:16 ff

DAY 124

Song of Songs 7:5 (NIV)
Your head crowns you like Mount Carmel. Your hair is like royal tapestry; the king is held captive by its tresses.

Psalm 45:8 (NIV)
All your robes are fragrant with myrrh and aloes and cassis, from the palaces adorned with ivory the music of strings makes you glad.

The words of the Psalmist echo very much the words of the Lover describing the Beloved. Psalm 45 is entitled a 'wedding song'; does this mean that fragrances have particular nuptial connotations? Or is it that they convey the language of romance of those days? When I take them as a love song applied to myself I find I erect barriers to stop them from reaching my emotions. There is a shame and embarrassment connected with receiving 'gushing' compliments. Is there an experience, a lie, something painful that is haunting me on this and preventing me from enjoying the fullness of who I am? Or is it saying that I am embarrassed by not being able to understand or explain the mystery? Even so, I am determined to understand!

Prayer & Contemplation:

"Lord, when I read these words and apply them to my own life, I can feel deep, inner squirms of shame, ridicule and embarrassment. Is there anything to be done about that? I know in my head You have taken all my sin and shame – but I don't always know that in my emotions. There is a definite and strong defence mechanism – one that seems like I can do nothing to prevent, one that it seems to present too big a risk to move out of.

"Open my heart to receive the good and the descriptive when spoken of me – by You and by others. Open my heart to feel the good of me, and from this place of confidence open my mouth to speak good of others... and then to dare even from a place of feeling awful about myself to still speak good of others."

DAY 125

Song of Songs 7:5b (NIV)
...the king is held captive by its tresses.

A king held captive by anything seems unlikely, but here is a king, one who has everything, being totally consumed by the hair of his beloved.

This draws me to the Sermon on the Mount where Jesus tells us that God knows the number of the hairs on our heads. Jesus is so entranced by us that He knows about each hair. If He knows about each hair, how much more will He long to know each thought, each experience, each heart-cry, each profound longing? Can we dare to believe that He not only longs to be that close but *is* that close? When we made that leap of faith, He entered every part of us, and now the mystery of faith is to dare to explore – to seek Him with all our hearts. Sometimes you may feel disappointed or that you cannot find Him, but that doesn't mean He is not there. The exploration is to find Him in the way He chooses to reveal Himself and not in the way we expect or demand that He be found. For me, so long as my hair is tidy and well cut, I don't much care about fashion, and therefore I find it hard to believe Jesus is interested in every hair. I could ignore this revelation He is giving because it is not where I'm looking, and I could leave these words and this meditation, stomping off, bemoaning the fact that Jesus has deserted me... Not so though. As I dare to look beyond that which I consider unimportant and I ask the Spirit to reveal Jesus to me, so I begin to sense the wonder of the almighty Son of God being interested even in all those hairs that have disappeared down the plughole after my shower this morning. If He cares for them, which I consider inconsequential, I find my spirit wandering into all the other areas that I consider similarly, and I am washed by the gentle love of understanding. This understanding has no words as such, but it gently caresses me, causing my eyes to search, and I find myself open-mouthed in awe at such care.

Prayer & Contemplation: *God is concerned with every detail in your life – even those you may consider insignificant. Are there areas of your life that you need to hand over to His care and concern today?*

DAY 126

Song of Songs 7:6 (NIV)
How beautiful you are and how pleasing, my love, with your delights!

Sometimes our English language seems so limited, and I feel tempted to read these words in French or Italian or other languages that seem to intrinsically hold love and charm in their form. Beautiful and pleasing! Pleasing and beautiful! How many ways are there to try to express what a heart feels and spiritual eyes see? 'Tis a mystery – and one which is doomed to remain hidden this side of Heaven. There is such a danger of familiarity breeding contempt with our limited language. We can read these words and gloss over them. Even putting them in context with what precedes and what follows, there is still a tendency to be blasé and to skim on, with our eyes looking for the next bit of novelty. When we do that we miss so much... and in the missing detract from the joys that follow.

Stop and enter quietly into some experience that has left you speechless! Depending on your personality, you may respond in various ways – anything from total wide-eyed stillness to cartwheeling whoops of glee! All these expressions are valid and acceptable to God. He is delighted you've noticed and received what He's been saying to you. As you responded so God, Almighty Creator, He responds too – in magnified and multiplied form! We are made in His image, and by His Spirit He lives inside. Choose to be consummated by His delight in you! Your natural adornment is beautiful and pleasing, and your inner soul... well... it is a delight! We don't have to dance the seven veils to attract his attention; we don't have to walk the catwalks of the world's chic fashion houses. We don't have to wax eloquently and lure Him in. He's there. He has already totally sacrificed Himself for your love. As we choose to love, to open ourselves, to explore ourselves and Him, so we will enter those wordless caverns of consummate love where everything else fades into oblivion.

Prayer & Contemplation: *Imagine Jesus with you, adoring you. The truth is, he sees you every moment as pleasing and beautiful.*

DAY 127

Song of Songs 7:7 (NASB)
Your stature is like a palm tree, And your breasts are like its clusters.

It doesn't take much imagination to conjure up this image. Even though they are not native of this land, in the temperate south palm trees are not unheard of out in the open, and even in the less-than-temperate north glasshouses will contain them. The image is of a tree tall and erect – not totally smooth in its trunk but straight and true and with all its potential for life at the top.

Whilst we don't doubt the Lover is conscious of the mind of the Beloved and the wealth contained therein, as we progress through the next few verses we can be certain that her mind is not the centre of his desires. There is a flame in his loins that is aching for fulfilment and driving him to the point of demanding satisfaction. We are left in no doubt that all his sensual and sexual being is completely alive. The point of consummation is not far away. The place of raw and naked self-giving is where they are headed. When that consummation is mutual, love rules; when it is only one who seeks consummation, lust rules. The former is the gift of union, the latter theft by rape. The former brings fulfilment of basic, God-given needs; the latter brings self-hatred and debasement as the basic God-given needs are ridden roughshod over.

This song, as it reaches its crescendo, will bring a response. The Lover has chosen to reveal himself in all his vulnerability; how will she respond? As we enter the last stanza of this ode to love, he risks all! One hint of rejection from her and he will be totally crushed.

Once again, let's stop and realise that Jesus makes Himself this vulnerable to us. Maybe for me as a woman that is more easily understood. I can understand that this description is flattery (in a positive sense!) and uplifting but I wonder how a man will receive such overtures from His Lord and Saviour. Maybe he doesn't or can't and this book of Song of Songs is not a Scripture for men to read! But I find that a hard opinion to accept – for all Scripture is for all people. I sense that in daring to bring a female interpretation to this Scripture I release the potential for men to begin to enter the reality of having the desire to be wooed and won; of knowing what it is like to be the focus of Jesus' attention in an emotional way; of entering into a new realm of fruitfulness and what it is to have another life inside them.

In a sexual union the male plants life into the female. He penetrates beyond himself and into another, something a female cannot do. The female is the receptacle of life, something a man cannot be. Yet spiritually both he and she are bearers and potential growers of the manifest life of God. As a man longs to bring life in another, such is the longing of God in both male and female. As a woman longs to carry life and hold life, such is the longing of God in both male and female. The intensity of unvoiced love for man to wife is a mirror of the demonstrated love from God to mankind. There is no greater 'wanting' than that God has for each of us. Ask the Spirit to reveal Jesus to you in all of this. Don't be afraid of the passion aroused; enjoy it with and in God, and use it as a springboard for appropriate use in the lives of those around. God still has laws set out for our behaviour. He will forgive our sins, but that is not carte-blanche to allow passions to rule indiscriminately. In giving us free will God loves us enough to ask us to choose to use these passions for His glory and the fulfilment of others and not solely for personal satisfaction. Sin corrupts and perverts – something the Beloved is all too aware of as we are reminded with her repeated warning to her friends. However, not allowing passion to rise for fear of sin means the enemy has won because he has only corrupted what God intended for good. There are ways of living a passionate and godly life that will bring glory to God.

Prayer & Contemplation: *What seed has God planted in your life? What does He want you to give birth to, spiritually? The miracle is that the process of forming a child does not require skill – only availability. God simply wants your life surrendered to His good purposes. There may be times of waiting, there may be birthing pains, but the birth will happen naturally and at the right time.*

DAY 128

Song of Songs 7:8a (NASB)
I said, 'I will climb the palm tree, I will take hold of its fruit stalks.'

As we join the couple at their most erotic and sensual moments – where desire has given full flow to its expression, where consummation reaches sublime heights – we could feel voyeuristic, or disgusted, or titillated, or tempted, or aroused, or prudish. A difficult task is to read these words and for a moment divorce our emotions from what our eyes receive. The Lover has acknowledged what he feels, and now he is declaring his chosen response to those feelings. His choice is action that will fully declare his feelings by deed; his choice is action that owns his expectations of being fulfilled. He believes that this 'palm tree' holds for him sublime consummation of who he is. With a sense of anticipation and wonder, he embarks on a new journey of discovery: discovery of self, discovery of her, discovery of life, discovery of relationship. He has reached the pinnacle of potential, and he waits for unknown wonders to be revealed.

Receive these as Jesus' words to us and they become almost incomprehensible. As a path into divine intimacy they are an open invitation to sheer wonder. Why should holy, sinless Son of God want anything to do with filthy, sinful me? Take that as a negative and we will shut the door and walk away, believing that it has "impossible" stamped across the doorway. Take that as a positive and we find the door flung open with the words "with God everything is possible" written on the threshold. The invitation is there to explore (and it will take eternity) the depths of the heart of God. The Lover of my soul bids me walk with Him, and each step of the way He will reveal more of Himself, more of me, and more of others. He lives in me and consequently I can expect to be loved and to give love in all its varieties, including the intimate, sensual and erotic in all purity.

When we allow our emotions to kick back in, often bad experiences or lies will be revealed. God's Word tells us we were made in His image, and as we choose to let the Holy Spirit do His refining work, even the worst and most damaging experience will no longer have power to hold us or defeat us. The Apostle Paul struggles with his sinful self in Romans chapter 7 and then starts chapter 8 with...

> *Therefore, there is now no condemnation for those who are in Christ Jesus.*

If we focus on what we consider to be wrong about the inclusion of these words from Song of Songs in Scripture, we will be consigning a pearl of great price to always be in the pigswill. So let's focus on how Jesus intended these words in our lives... and discover! For each of us the discovery will be different, but it will always be some aspect of the character of Jesus for that is the Spirit's primary task. As we discover the character of Jesus, so we find our own character being polished to reflect His glory.

Prayer & Contemplation: *Begin your discovery today. Ask Jesus to show you today how He wants to be involved in your life. Allow Him access to your heart. Let Him speak what seems impossible and then, in His time and way, make it a reality!*

DAY 129

Song of Songs 7:8b-9a (NASB)
Oh, may your breasts be like clusters of the vine, and the fragrance of your breath like apples, and your mouth like the best wine!

Pause silently and contemplate the privilege of enjoining the deep, intimate moments as two souls unite. We tiptoe, breathless and spellbound, awed by this so proud and powerful Lover laying himself, his desires and his actions bare. This is not a place for girly giggles nor adult humour's smutty sniggers. This is an intense moment of union where each soul completes the other.

This is a place most males long for and fear at the same time. It takes them back to their mother's breast where they were totally nurtured and completely secure. Here the man lays down his responsibilities and regains his childlike vulnerability, where he is unable to fend for himself and he thrives only through maternal sustenance. This is a place of fear for it opens him to attack, abuse and humiliation. His defences are down! A look, a word, a sound, an action or the lack thereof, could bring total destruction of self. In his dominant role in a patriarchal society he commits himself to the weakest of positions, to possibly be manipulated, arrested or destroyed by a woman. Shame would prod at him from all quarters, but love is so strong that he is prepared to risk all that for a taste of the promise that reciprocated love will bring him.

Many would argue that it is extremely foolish to make oneself this vulnerable to anyone – that it is asking for trouble. Such comments derive from personal pain; we live with conditional love... and we die from conditional love.

Prayer & Contemplation: *Jesus is speaking to us with these words – His Bride – the Church corporately, you and me individually. Can such longings reside in the heart of the Son of Almighty Creator God? Yes, and even more, for as we've already observed language is such a poor expression of all that is good, holy and pure in God.*

DAY 130

Song of Songs 7:8b-9a (NASB)
Oh, may your breasts be like clusters of the vine, and the fragrance of your breath like apples, and your mouth like the best wine!

Isaiah 49:15 (NIV)
Can a mother forget the baby at her breast, and have no compassion on the child she had borne? Though she may forget, I will never forget you.

Until I had my own children I never considered myself maternal. You would not, and still won't, catch me billing and cooing over the pram of a new baby – except my own. The sheer wonder of life – giving life and sustaining life – is a powerful experience. Those mothers who, for whatever reason, never get to hold their own child know the heartache and despair that stays with them forever. For me, even in the early hours, the greatest joy was to cuddle my baby close and feed her. Such a deep contentment I have never found. Many other satisfactions are found in watching the child grow and find independence, but they don't hold a torch to being the sole provider. I don't find it all that farfetched to believe God finds such contentment in me. When I lay down my struggle for independence and doing things my way and I choose to clamber into His arms, there is not only contentment, satisfaction and replenishment for me but it is also a place where, just by being me, I give to Him and He is completed and satisfied.

I can understand why the Lover uses fruitfulness and intoxication as emblems in his description; these are the closest description of the relaxation, freedom and abandonment that deeply-giving relationship affords. Whilst we take it in our earthly relationships and get glimpses of it in our earthly worship, it is nothing like the indescribable consummation that awaits in the Father's house. We will know what it is to be totally stilled and totally active; totally alive, yet completely empty – and paradoxically full.

Prayer & Contemplation: *If you have parented a child, know that the natural love-bond you experience is just a dim reflection of how the Father loves you. Ask Him to deepen your revelation of His love.*

DAY 131

Song of Songs 7:9b (NIV)
May the wine go straight to my beloved, flowing gently over lips and teeth.

"But soft what light through yonder window breaks..."[29]

The whispered words of Romeo, as Juliet moves into view, herald for me the attitude of wonder as we hear the Beloved's reply to the Lover's poured-out heart. In the heightened moment between him becoming silent and her lifting her voice to respond is great suspense. What will her reply be? Which way will the scales tip? Will she? Won't she? Tantalised, our eternal wait is ended.

Sublimely her response is all we – and he – have hoped for, and more even. For we forget so quickly that love is so much more far reaching than our limited imagination will allow it to be.

The intoxicating gift of 'all that she is' is surrendered willingly to him. There is no deviation; it's for him alone. All that she has is to pass through his senses, to be absorbed into him. It is the mystical union of two becoming one in marriage – initiated at the beginning of time by our Creator, who knows what is best for us – the metamorphosis of two separate souls, remaining separate identities yet making one completely new whole.

Prayer & Contemplation: Ask God to show you any area of your life that has not yet been surrendered to Him. Make the step today to invite Him into any closed area, and trust Him as your Lord and Lover.

---

[29] Romeo & Juliet Act 2 Scene 2

DAY 132

Song of Songs 7:10 (NASB)
I am my beloved's, and his desire is for me.

If there remained an iota of doubt in our minds that the Beloved is fully engrossed and besotted with the Lover then here is the statement that unequivocally casts it out.

Here we have a statement of fact and a statement of intent mingled together.

Fact: she declares her allegiance and her knowledge of ownership. She belongs: such security, such satisfaction, such fulfilment. She has moved from her background of abuse and mistreatment, where fear reigned, to her present and future of lavish love and complete security.

Intent: she declares his desire for her – and with this she declares her intention to enter into all the discovery, revelation and mystery of what his desire will be and who she will discover him to be. She has discovered the awe of finding in his desire her own desires awakened. This is not just a one-way journey; it is a two-way journey of two souls experiencing each other, the world around them and their God.

As Jesus' Beloved, can we voice the same words with such hope and potential, knowing Jesus is not a 'one-off event'? This is no 'been there, done that, worn out the T-shirt' relationship. This is forever – a 'forever friendship' where love continually strips back the layers of our self-defence to bring us deeper into the mystery of eternal, unconditional love.

We see childlike faith at work as the Beloved reverts to childhood in order to have restored to her the joy of love and life that both she and others stole from her. Our Lover's desire for us is so intent that He will stop at nothing to draw our attention to it. Two thousand years ago He made the most public declaration of love this world has ever seen. He made it at His birth with His choice to be trapped in time and in a womb. He made it in the unknown years when He chose to remain in obscurity just being human. He made it in His ministry when He was reviled, rejected and misunderstood. He made it on Calvary: "Father, forgive!"[30] He made it in the Easter garden. He made it on the Mount of Ascension. He made it on the day of Pentecost. He makes it each time a new soul opens and lets Him in. He makes it each time a soul's door is slammed in His face.

Prayer & Contemplation: *How wide are your eyes? How wide are the eyes of your soul? With all your childlike capacity, ask Him how much desire He has for you, then sit quietly and listen with your soul to the response He gives. Don't rush! Wait! Will your response be similar to the Beloved's?*

---

[30] Luke 23:34

DAY 133

Song of Songs 7:11 (NASB)
Come, my beloved, let us go out into the country, let us spend the night in the villages[31].

This and the following verses reveal the joy bubbling excitedly from the Beloved's lips. Exuberance underlines every word. This is no pleading, beseeching request. This is a 'grab by the hand and whisk off with gay abandon' response. She is overwhelmed and is unable to contain all that she feels. "Quick! Let's go and grab the moment!" Carpe Diem! Who else but lovers would think about spending the night in the henna bushes? (I don't understand Hebrew, but the romantic in me thinks this should be translated 'henna bushes' and not 'villages'; with all the talk of fragrance, colour and texture, 'villages' just doesn't fit the bill!)

When was the last time you did this to the person you love? When was the last time you did this to Jesus? What?! Are you aghast at the suggestion? Too grown up for things like that?! "What would the neighbours think?" "What would the congregation think?" "Jesus wouldn't want me to do that!" How do you know? Have you asked Him? What are our expectations of how Jesus would behave? Read the Gospels; listen to Jesus tell parables! Would He have told them in a dull monotone? Or would there have been a twinkle in His eye, a knowing look on his face? He is the loving, laughing, life-giving Son of God who promises abundance and lavishness – and forever.

The Lover has taken a 'sow's ear' and is making a beautiful silk purse – a purse that contains not coins, gold nor jewels but joy, hope and love, all wrapped up in a restored soul. Dare we refuse to go through the same process?

If the Lover and the Beloved spent the night in the henna bushes, wouldn't everyone know about it? Yes! We would find several attitudes in response to that – everything from the strong desire to frown, condemn, criticise and castigate, to saying, "We wish we were in your shoes!" Is it possible to move from one end to the other? Yes! And unfortunately most of us opt for going the wrong way; in our desire for perceived maturity we easily denounce such action, and in

---

[31] Or henna bushes

the denouncing we slam the door shut on such 'childish and immature' behaviour, forgetting that Jesus said:

Matthew 18:3 (NIV)
Unless you change and become like little children you will never enter the Kingdom of Heaven.

We are in danger of becoming foolishly over-mature. Let's throw off the shackles we've placed on ourselves (or had placed on us) and run with the Beloved and her Lover to the vineyards!

Prayer & Contemplation: *Is your relationship with Jesus fun and childlike? Or is it distant and severe? There is a time to be serious, a time for soberness and a time for mourning. But every relationship also needs to be seasoned with intimacy, laughter and pleasure. Talk with Jesus about your relationship today. What does it need? How can you achieve that?*

Day 134

Song of Songs 7:12 (NIV)
Let us go early to the vineyards to see if the vines have budded, if their blossoms have opened, and if the pomegranates are in bloom – there I will give you my love.

The Beloved returns to the familiar, that which is so much part of her – the vineyard. I don't suppose for one minute that here she is referring to her brothers' vineyards. No, this must be reference to her vineyard – so long neglected but being tenderly nurtured and cherished back to fruitfulness. Real vineyard or soul vineyard, it doesn't really matter, for the invite is for the Lover to own both. We catch the sense of promise, hope and anticipation in the Beloved's voice; this is no vain drumming up of forlorn hope, this is knowledge of a sure and certain fruitfulness. The vineyard will have been her place of safety, her retreat from the beatings and abuse in the family; it is now made even more secure by the nurture of the Lover. He is now so much part of her that fruitfulness is guaranteed.

Imagine the fragrance of being surrounded by buds, flowers, blossoms and fruit and in the intensity and headiness of all that she will give her love: all of her, holding nothing back, unreservedly; she belongs to her Lover and that is sheer delight.

This challenges us to ask how delighted and wholehearted we are to meet with our Lover and be fruitful with Him. Does prayer, the place of meeting, inspire us to want to drag Jesus off with gay abandon? Or does this place feels dreary and full of drudgery and duty laden? How we need to ask the Holy Spirit to show us Jesus and all His desires so that the place of prayer becomes a place we can't wait to get to and that we don't want to be dragged away from – rather than vice-versa!

I can't imagine that the Beloved couldn't wait to leave the vineyard; rather, time would have been insignificant, other duties put out of mind. All that mattered was being there with Him. He pervaded all. Her focus was on Him alone. The sole purpose of life was to be with Him. All she did was secondary to being able to love Him. This love was complete – filial, erotic and 'agape' – and the mystery was (and is) that even in its completeness there was still more to discover.

The more we think we know God the more convinced we become that we know so little. Time-bound bodies, minds and spirits can only glimpse eternity and have their appetites whetted to keep searching. We are stilled into being, from whence we are stirred into action. Being must come first; otherwise action loses its eternal dimension.

Prayer & Contemplation: *Has your prayer life become one of ritual or one of daily relationship? Are there religious habits that need to be broken in order to infuse life back into your times with your Lover? Ask the Holy Spirit to increase your revelation of Jesus and His desires today.*

DAY 135

Song of Songs 7:13 (KJV)
The mandrakes give a smell, and at our gates are all manner of pleasant fruits, new and old, which I have laid up for thee, O my beloved.

Mandrakes are love apples! They are found also in Genesis 30 as a hire fee from Leah and Rachel in return for Jacob sleeping with them. Perhaps these are considered to be an aphrodisiac.

The revelation of desire continues as each word drops from the Beloved's lips. Every opportunity and encouragement to feast and be satisfied is offered to the Lover. She knows there are old delicacies, ones which he and probably others have tasted, but also she knows that there is so much new to explore and enjoy. We sense that she knows this adventure has only just begun and holds the promise of so much. Although much may have been stolen from her, she also knows that she has, through sacrifice, been able to save much to give to him, the pure lover of her soul.

When we do not keep ourselves until after marriage, there is huge sadness at what is lost, thrown away even, by such a casual approach to our sexual desires. I sense the Beloved would know some of this sadness, and it would be easy to wallow in the might-have-been and the if-only; to listen to the voice that says, "You've blown it! You can never know true intimacy!"; to hear the whispers of longing and to bring it under remorse, guilt and shame… But God specialises in taking the rotten, bad, poor, blind and revealing His glory in them. It may not be easy, nor will it be without pain – emotional and soul pain – but there is a part of us where only God fits. When with His help and healing we clear out the clutter we've tried to bring in there, He will pour in His glory. Our earthen vessel will glow with the energy that only He can give as we receive grace upon grace from His hand. It is an upward path, slippery and strewn with boulders. We may often slip and slide back. We may feel like giving up, and each time we feel that way there will be a choice: listen to God's voice or listen to lies! Even when we listen to lies, the voice of God will keep whispering; the door to intimacy with Him is never locked and sealed, but the handle is on our side. When God restores, things are never the same again. They are always better – better, that is, from His perspective because we will have become more like Jesus and God's heart will sing even more loudly over us. This is the Beloved speaking to the Lover; what we must realise is that God has so much more to give and reveal than we can never know.

Prayer & Contemplation: *Ask the Holy Spirit to reveal any clutter in your life that needs to be cleared out. Confess these things, and then invite Jesus to come and dwell in the space you have made. Ask the Holy Spirit to fill you afresh.*

DAY 136

Song of Songs 8:1 (NIV)
If only you were to me like a brother, who was nursed at my mother's breasts! Then, if I found you outside, I would kiss you, and no one would despise me.

The Lover has brought so much life, affirmation and hope into the Beloved's soul, yet still she is fearful. Her mind is making ways for her to be intimate with the Lover without the fear of reprimand, humiliation or correction from those around her of whom she is still concerned.

"If only..." How many times have we voiced those words? And if we've voiced them out loud that many times, how many more times have we thought them? *If only* I'd been born at a different time, in a different place, to a different family. *If only* I hadn't said or done a certain thing.

This "if only" helps us to realise just how human the Beloved is; because she appears in Scripture, it's all too easy to view her through a holy haze. This "if only" brings us into her and opens the way for us to realise that it is okay for us to identify with her in all her longings and to receive the replies from the Lover as our own.

If only the Lover were her brother... She has brothers and knows how to behave with them. Experience has laid down a chart for her to follow, one that's acceptable and keeps her 'safe'. But he's not; he's her lover – totally unrelated. And as she experiences the thrill of a new intimacy she faces her inner fear of getting it wrong – wrong in her own eyes (bad enough) but also in His eyes ("Horror of horrors! He might not love me anymore!") This is the exploration of intimacy Jesus invites us to. Will we long to keep safe and relate in the tried, familiar and acceptable ways, or will we walk the path of unconditional love? There is nothing we can do, say or think that will separate us from Him as far as He's concerned. The only thing to prevent us entering into all His fullness is our own unwillingness to dare.

The Beloved knows what it is to be despised. She also knows what it is to despise herself, although she may not recognise the fact. She hates being despised and is looking everywhere for a way to make things safe so that she will not be despised in this relationship. *If only she could make it safe… but she can't; only the Lover can. As we shall see later, He is offering a safety that feels totally unsafe to her! If only* he were nursed at her mother's breasts, as family, then in her mind there would be safety. However, He is being nursed at her breasts, and she feels everyone's eyes are on her and judging her critically!

Prayer & Contemplation: *Do you play "if only" on Jesus? Do you try to keep yourself safe by the 'rules of acceptability' that you have laid down?*

DAY 137

Song of Songs 8:1b (NIV)
...Then, if I found you outside, I would kiss you, and no-one would despise me.

Two questions come to mind. Was the Beloved ever kissed? Was she ever kissed in public?

Social custom in the Middle East is very different even today, and therefore it is not unreasonable to presume there were differences when this was written. I wonder if the Beloved had sometime in the past overstepped protocol. I sense a deep longing in the Beloved to be publicly affirmed and accepted – why else the underlying fear of being despised? She knows what 'despicable' feels like. I suspect it's a label she has at least placed on herself from others' reaction to her, if not one that others have given in her hearing. How isolating it is to be despised. How self-destructive it is to despise oneself. There is venom in the word that feels as if it can be spat a great distance with deadly accuracy; not leaving an outward mark but inwardly corrosive, destroying the soul.

Joy wants to demonstrate the love and freedom she's found. Fear still taunts her with doubts, especially of what others might think. This gets too near the mark for so many of us. We piously make choices for the 'good of another' but hidden underneath is the motive of self-protection: anything to keep me safe, anything to sweeten this person and make them still love me! All the time we make choices based on the inner question, "Will you still love me?"

Prayer & Contemplation: *Ask God to show you the motives behind the choices you make for others' good. Are they truly out of selfless love? Do you hope to win their favour? Would you feel offended if your kind action was not recognised? Do you try to protect yourself by not making others aware of your own needs and desires?*

Day 138

Song of Songs 8:2 (KJV)
I would lead thee, and bring thee into my mother's house, who would instruct me: I would cause thee to drink of spiced wine of the juice of my pomegranate.

What affirmation and reassurance of safety, tenderness and lavish love! There would be no fear of the Lover getting lost for the Beloved would lead the way; no having to remember intricate directions, no risk of guesswork, but a sure and certain guide who would know every step intimately.

"...into my mother's house" suggests the Beloved longs to reveal everything feminine about herself, to bring the revelation of all she knows about her sensuality and sexuality. The wonder will be that she will find so much more, because until consummation and connection with all that is masculine in him, she is still missing vital ingredients that even her mother could not give her. She may have told her, described as vividly and articulately as possible, but that would not be a patch on the fulfilment she will find in union with him. The Beloved is telling him that she longs to give him all that she knows she is, and to risk finding more, thereby entering new realms of personhood thus far denied her. This is vulnerability at its utmost. This is giving beyond known limits. This is entering realms thus far only dreamed of... and it will be intoxicating beyond a concoction of spiced wine with the juice of pomegranates.

Prayer & Contemplation: *Today, trust yourself to Him who loves so profoundly, so that you too can enter the kingdom of intimacy where you and He become one; two different people, yet filled with the aura of eternity. Enter the sublime. Drink deep, for the cup will never run dry! Be sustained for the journey, for as much as we might desire, we cannot remain here.*

DAY 139

Song of Songs 8:3-5a (NASB)

Let his left hand be under my head and his right hand embrace me. I want you to swear, O daughters of Jerusalem, do not arouse or awaken my love until she pleases. [Friends] Who is this coming up from the wilderness leaning on her beloved?

In the overall plot, this is hard to put into context. We've read the most erotic descriptions from Lover and Beloved, and the friends interject. It seems that they haven't been party to all that's gone on, and yet the Beloved just spoke to them. Placing the sequence of events is difficult, especially when it is not always obvious where people are when the words are spoken. Why, when the Beloved has so obviously addressed them, are they questioning who is coming, as if the Beloved would be a long way off?

"Who is coming up from the wilderness?" is a question the Beloved has already asked (3:6)! She was observing the Lover with all his fighting men; now the friends observe her, leaning on her Lover. Is she leaning as in 'exhausted, no strength left'? Or is she leaning as in 'totally enraptured, can't take her eyes off him'? It could be either or both.

The wilderness seems such a significant place…

Prayer & Contemplation: *Do you feel as though you are in a wilderness in your life right now? Although you may feel tired, hungry and unfulfilled, the wilderness is part of the journey to the Promised Land. Choose to walk through this time leaning on your Lover. Even if you do not sense God's presence, trust in His closeness and faithfulness. He will walk through this period with you.*

DAY 140

Song of Songs 8:5b (NKJV)
*I awakened you under the apple tree. There your mother brought
you forth; there she who bore you brought you forth.*

"…under the apple tree" sounds a really safe and familiar place –
special and soul-touching; one of those places where just to think of it
causes well-being to spread around the body and anticipation to rise.
Surely we are, as the Psalmist says, "fearfully and wonderfully
made,"[32] when a mere memory or thought can bring such good to
our lives.

Secret places are places we only share with those who will
treasure their memory and enhance their beauty for us. We would not
want to risk anyone desecrating it, for in its destruction they would
destroy our very selves. The Beloved has been welcomed into the
Lover's secret place. Is it a real place that they've visited, or is it just
the memory? One wonders about all that the Lover has told her
about it and the sort of relationship he must have had with his
mother for her to tell him such intimate details of his conception and
birth! It brings to mind all those childlike questions of "Where did I
come from?" and those equally embarrassed moments as the parent
wrestles with just how much to feed into an inquisitive yet sensitive
mind. Somehow the naivety of childhood gets squashed out of us; we
catch the adult embarrassment and stop asking the childlike
questions.

The more I ponder the apple tree, the more overwhelming the
sense of fruitfulness, sweetness and delicacy comes. I could place
myself under a typical British apple tree here – on a balmy spring day,
lying on a bed of soft green grass, gazing up at the blue sky through
the leafy branches, watching the delicately coloured blossom dancing
as it is caressed by the warm breeze to the accompaniment of the
melody of the bees as they gather nectar. I sense the love that flows as
a child is conceived; the intensity of the love focus as the individuals
turn outwards, as the adornment of nature calls them to the
realisation of One greater than they who has created them to enjoy
Him and each other with such consummate delight.

---

[32] Psalm 139:14

Even the painful anguish of labour gives way with ease to the delight of the fullness of new life. Under the apple tree is a place of realisation of potential: one generation giving potential to the next and now the next expecting to propagate that potential.

Prayer & Contemplation: *Perhaps you are spiritually giving birth to something that God has planted in your heart. You may feel that others don't notice or understand the labour pains you are experiencing in bringing God's plans to fruition; you are in a secret place. But Jesus, your Lover, is with you in that place, and your current pain will be replaced with joy in time. Keep your eyes fixed on Him and on His promises.*

DAY 141

Song of Songs 8:6 (NKJV)

Set me as a seal upon your heart, as a seal upon your arm; for love is as strong as death, jealousy as cruel as the grave [its ardour unyielding as Sheol]; its flames are flames of fire, a most vehement flame [like the very flame of God].

The intensity of this verse always reaches deep into my core. For many years I read it as Jesus asking me to place Him as a seal on my heart! That seems logical, for my heart is "deceitful above all things"[33] and is in great need of a shield, particularly the shield that is Jesus. It was only recently that I realised that this is the *Beloved* speaking and therefore, in the allegorical sense, represents me asking Jesus to put me as a seal over *His* heart and arm! I cannot fathom why He should want to do that, but I know that is what He wants! I look in myself and see nothing of worth that should merit making me a seal, a stamp of ownership, but the longer I walk with Him the more I appreciate the duality of ownership and that somehow He shines out through my declaration of owning Him. I cannot own Him nor possess Him, as if to clutch Him to myself – but I *can* own Him and possess Him in an open hand. This is the place of security, of total belonging, in that I can give all away and still be assured that I possess all! How slow I am to grasp this! How fallen I am because I still so readily grasp selfishly and sinfully what has been so freely given. These words convince me and convict me at the same time. I rise up to worship with all that I am; I fall down to repent of all that I am not!

A seal is an individual's unique mark! The psalmist echoes this when he understands God telling him that he is engraved on the palm of God's hands[34]; whatever God touches, He leaves the mark of us in His prints!

The jealousy referred to in this verse is jealousy in its positive sense – as in "I, the Lord your God, am a jealous God."[35] For us, where jealousy is only a painful, negative and destructive emotion, it

---

[33] Jeremiah 17:19
[34] Isaiah 49:16
[35] Exodus 20:5

is hard to grapple with love and jealousy in the same sentence. This is where the word 'ardour' helps, although it is a word not much used today and probably doesn't carry the passionate force that it would have done generations ago. The verse is saying is that there is nothing – not even death – that can destroy or steal the strength of passion the Beloved feels. It burns; it consumes; it on the one hand feels totally destructive and yet with all the power of purification it only destroys the unnecessary whilst it enhances and hones the best and most beautiful.

When we come face-to-face with the love of Jesus it is the most painful and frightening experience ever. Everything that we thought we were or had just crumbles to ash and is blown away. All those good deeds, good thoughts and hours of sacrifice are reduced to blackened charcoal... But look hard and there will be gold dust that remains – the gold of the time spent alone with Jesus.

Prayer & Contemplation: *The Refiner's fire is a place we tend to avoid – the flame of the Lord seems too much – but without it all we do is build sandcastles on the beach to be washed away by the next turn of the tide. Thank God today for His refining work in Your life.*

DAY 142

Song of Songs 8:7 (NKJV)
Many waters cannot quench love, nor can the floods drown it. If a man would give for love all the wealth of his house, it would be utterly despised.

When love blazes, not even the most ferocious of floods can wash it away. The thirst love gives cannot be satisfied. It remains. Jesus picked up this when He talked to the Samaritan woman at the well:

John 4:13
Whoever drinks of the water I shall give will never thirst again!

Will they *never* feel thirsty? They will if they do not always go to the best place to drink. But they never *need* feel thirsty again for the supply from Heaven is unending, eternal! The Beloved understood this, and one of our life's aims must be to attain a place where we never feel thirsty, an instinctive place where whenever we need to know we're loved we will always turn to Jesus. This is tough though; for the world clamours and attracts our attention, and we quickly and without knowing divert from the best path.

Love, like the Beloved has discovered, is again highlighted by Jesus in His parable of the pearl of great price.[36] Surely everyone thought the man in Jesus' story was barking mad to sell everything and to borrow as well to buy this field! Yet they didn't know what he'd discovered. So many treat Jesus' followers the same way. Scorn and humiliation are often the lot when we testify to being a Christian or going to church. Jesus knows about scorn and humiliation!

You took all my sin and shame when You died and rose again.[37]

Spat on, mocked, beaten, taunted and yet still so full of love. We have so much still to learn!

---

[36] Matthew 13:45

[37] From the song "You laid aside your majesty"; words and music by *Noel Richards;* (c) Copyright 1985 *Thankyou Music* / Adm. by *worshiptogether.com Songs* excl. UK & Europe, adm. by *Kingswaysongs,* a division of *David C Cook;* tym@kingsway.co.uk. Used by permission.

Sometimes I will give all the wealth of my house for love like this, but only fleetingly! How much further I still have to walk! What about you?

Prayer & Contemplation: *Do you feel spiritually thirsty? Are you in a dry place right now? Choose to come to Jesus, the source of living water. Ask Him for water, and He will fill you.*

DAY 143

Song of Songs 8:6-7 (NKJV)

Set me as a seal upon your heart, as a seal upon your arm; for love is as strong as death, jealousy as cruel as the grave; its flames are flames of fire, a most vehement flame. Many waters cannot quench love, nor can the floods drown it. If a man would give for love all the wealth of his house, it would be utterly despised.

The most amazing thing about these words is that it is the Beloved who speaks them. So often they're read like a shield of protection – a command to us to put Jesus on our arms as protection, whereas this is the Beloved asking to be put on *His* arm, on *His* heart. A seal is a mark of belonging! It is only to be opened by the named recipient! It indicates an official document, usually binding!

The Beloved recognises that there is nothing she can do to buy the Lover's love, but she knows that it is something she would give her entire wealth for. She has tasted the full riches of unconditional love, and there is no way she is going to let it go! How often I taste the sweetness of my Lord's love and then am fecklessly drawn away by someone or something else that lures me. How fickle I can be!

Prayer & Contemplation:

"Lord, many rivers cannot quench Your love, and yet it seems that a mere trickle of water can wash my memory of it! Busy-ness and tiredness are two of the chief culprits when it comes to me forgetting where my focus should be, and before long I make myself the centre of my love and drift into 'pity-party' mode. Why You don't give up on me is beyond me! But these words tell me why You don't give up – because Your love took You to death and back, and You're not about to negate Your sacrifice by human fickleness. Your love burns so intensely that it sets out to reclaim me!"

DAY 144

Song of Songs 8:8 (NLT)
We have a little sister too young to have breasts. What will we do for our sister if someone asks to marry her?

The friends get caught up in the overflow of love as it gushes forth from the Beloved's soul. It's almost as if they realise that they may have missed out on all she's describing but don't want those loved by them to miss out as well. They talk of a young girl, pre-puberty, with the world at her feet – innocence personified with rich potential to find love but equally likely to be soiled and sullied by the world so that she misses out.

They long to be able to do something to prevent her from either being destroyed before she gets that far or from destroying herself by her choices.

I remember my "too young to have breasts" days – junior school days when already I was discovering that my self-esteem was well annihilated. Even in such youth I had shut myself away, living a self-protected life... to such an extent that the prison I locked myself inside became 'home' and the world of wonder in who I am became the place of fear.

Prayer & Contemplation: *Which word better describes how you feel about yourself – wonder or fear? Ask Jesus to share with you some of the wonder He experiences when He thinks of you. Seek forgiveness for the barriers you have raised around your heart, and forgive those who have caused the fear. Thank God for the way He has created you and that His creation is perfect.*

DAY 145

Song of Songs 8:9-10
If she is a wall, we will build towers of silver on her. If she is a door, we will enclose her with panels of cedar. [Beloved] I am a wall, and my breasts are like towers. Thus I have become in his eyes like one bringing contentment.

To me the friends' response and plan seems safe and welcoming, and yet I hear a voice echo deep within; it says, "Set her free! Don't close her up!" *If* she is a wall... *If* she is a door... What if she's neither? What if she's a garden, a jewel, an ocean? I know silver and cedar are precious and honoured and sought after, but they are also heavy, cumbersome and containing. I understand that they don't want her to risk corruption and thereby lose herself, but when we are protected we never find out if we can fly!

Was the Beloved listening to the friends? Maybe with only half an ear for she's picked up on the word 'wall'. Like a trigger it has shot her thoughts off at a tangent. She *is* a wall, to be scaled, to be hid behind, to find protection. Those towers of silver have become her breasts, everything precious and life-sustaining given for her Lover. She has reached a place of knowing, that recognises his contentment and the part she plays in it, but also finds her own contentment and fulfilment. It is reciprocal; it is not his contentment at the price of hers. As he is content to be with her and in her, so she is content to be with him and in him. As she is content to be with him and in him, so he is content to be with her and in her. The ebb and flow of love multiplies and magnifies, and from its overflow others are refreshed.

There are idyllic times when I know how that feels. I am content with Jesus and, amazingly, He is content with me. The truth is that I can stay in this place. The reality is that I so readily get drawn away; I become discontented with my lot, angry with the path God has chosen for me, and I spoil the party. Jesus never becomes discontented with me. He encourages me to change, but He doesn't stop loving me if I don't, won't or can't. That's grace.

Prayer & Contemplation: *Do you keep yourself pure for Jesus or allow things in your life (habits, thoughts, etc) that take your focus away from Him? Repent of those things and make Him Lord again.*

DAY 146

Song of Songs 8:11 (NKJV)
Solomon had a vineyard at Baal Hamon; he leased the vineyard to keepers; everyone was to bring for its fruit a thousand silver coins.

Baal Hamon means 'land of the multitude' and is a place in Mount Ephrah near Samaria. Ephraim means 'doubly fruitful'. What does the name tell us about Solomon's vineyard? The land is rich, prosperous and plentiful. Solomon was so wealthy he could afford to let such property to tenants rather than work it himself. He either had so much property that he couldn't manage it all himself or he was generous and gave others the opportunity for purpose in their lives. Yes, they had to pay a substantial rent, but they would live full lives rather than beggars' lives.

We see the plenty of all the Beloved describes but must bear in mind that this verse is there mainly as a comparison to what the Beloved is about to say…

Prayer & Contemplation: *Money and the desire to maintain a certain level of prosperity can easily distract us from the Kingdom of God. But Jesus encouraged us to store up treasures in heaven and earn heavenly rewards. Jesus' vineyards are for Him to give as He chooses, but He is looking for trustworthy servants. How can you store up more treasure in heaven?*

DAY 147

Song of Songs 8:12 (NLT)
But my vineyard is mine to give, and Solomon need not pay a thousand pieces of silver. But I will give two hundred pieces to those who care for its vines.

What a contrast from 1:6 when the Beloved considered her own vineyard as worth nothing. She had neglected it because of pressure from others. She looked at it then and saw nothing but worthlessness; she looks at it now and sees the sheer bounty of it. In the metaphorical sense she describes herself. We have been privileged to share the journey into worth with her – from the desolation of nothingness to the generosity of wholeness. She knows who she is and that all this is a gift to her Lover. Although value in shekels is placed on it, that is nothing compared with the infinite worth of a free soul, no longer abandoned to the prison of dark despair but freed to soar on the sublime wings of unconditional love.

This is a journey we too can choose to take – a lifetime's journey. So many of us start well, but we turn off into a friendly cul-de-sac and spend the rest of our time there, either oblivious to what else could be or incarcerated by our own set of fears. The voice of Joshua challenges us down the years: "Choose you this day..."[38] and the voice of Jesus beckons us into the Truth who will set us free...[39]

Prayer & Contemplation: *Are you still running the race for Christ? Or have you taken a detour or found a comfortable spot to rest? If so, come back to the Cross. As you remember the price Jesus paid for you, choose to live one hundred per cent for Him once again.*

---

[38] Joshua 24:15
[39] John 8:32

DAY 148

Song of Songs 8:13 (NIV)
You who dwell in the gardens with friends in attendance, let me hear your voice!

As the Lover wants to hear the Beloved, so Jesus wants to hear your voice. I wonder what He'd like to hear you say.

Despite the request to hear her voice, this is a place of deep, deep silence, a community of souls where words are superfluous. The Lover just wants to be with the Beloved and to know her. In this dwelling place there is total security; she could say the very best, the most erotic, the worst tragedy, or the most heinous confession, and she knows she will be safe. It would be enough that the Lover is totally for her, but there is a hint here that applies to the friends too. Nothing she says, acknowledges, confesses or longs for will stop them from loving her and wanting to be with her.

In these idyllic gardens she is free to roam, to frolic, to play, to run, to be still. The beauty of the surroundings is only there to enhance further her beauty. The fragrance of the flowers magnifies her perfume. The taste of the fruit multiplies her fruitfulness.

Now enter with me the depths of Jesus speaking those words to us! How do you feel? Awed? Frightened? Embarrassed? The first time I read these words I couldn't believe them, and I tried to ponder Jesus' reaction to all the awful things I might say or his reaction to my stumbling efforts to extol Him! It took a very long time and lots of encouragement from my friends to believe that Jesus longed to hear whatever I said to Him. If it was awful and sinful, He already knew about it! He'd felt the weight of it all on Calvary. If it was faltering praise, He would look with delight as a parent delights in their child's efforts. If it was dumping my feelings, He would be like my husband or my friends. Yes, in my mind I comprehended the truth of Jesus knowing all about me, but I could not absorb that in how I related to Him. Slowly, slowly, through much love, patience, challenge and action, I have walked into the fullness of all that this means... but this is 'present continuous' for I continue to walk into it all. I am full but I can be fuller. Is that a physical impossibility? Try filling a balloon with air. When is it full? After the first puff of breath blows it to its first point of resistance? When it's as blown up as you dare blow it? Or could more be squeezed in? Our souls are like that. The more we stop resisting Jesus, the greater the capacity there is to expand and hold more of Him. The more rubbish we speak out, the greater space there will be for Him to enter. As our faith grows bigger, He'll be there to fill us.

Prayer & Contemplation: *Speak to Jesus often – silently / out loud; on your own / with friends. A real friend will love you like Jesus, so whatever the rubbish they hear they'll still be there. Contrary to logical belief, it seems the more we describe how rotten we are, the more they seem to love us. Find someone who loves you and try it. You'll be amazed at how much of Jesus you'll see in them and how much of Jesus you'll find in yourself. Remember, love is a choice, and your friend has chosen you.*

DAY 149

Song of Songs 8:14 (NASB)
Hurry, my beloved, and be like a gazelle or a young stag on the mountains of spices.

This is the Beloved's response to the last words of the Lover.

Four words: 'Lord, I love you!' Why do they sometimes stick in my throat? In those times I can write them; I can say them in my heart... but my voice is silent... So simple: the struggle fades into insignificance as I breathe Jesus' name in and out. I give my life-breath out by speaking and receive His life-breath in again.

My heart pounds, and I feel like a young doe, breathless before Him. I clamber on the spice-laden mountains, drink in the heady fragrance and receive the healing life that spice balm brings... but more than that, I receive His very breath. It brings life again to dead and dying places.

With one breath He restores the lushness to this part of the garden. And as I am on the mountain I am aware of the waterfall. There has to be height for the water to fall from, and so the boundaries of the garden are enlarged to include not just the flat places but the heights as well, all life in one garden – the river, the heights, the luscious places, the fragrant places and places fit for human habitation; the walls are repaired and the streets are restored.

Prayer & Contemplation:

"You choose to dwell in my garden, Lord. By simple utterance of those four simple words – Lord, I love you – a whole new panorama comes into view, and acres more land are reclaimed for Your occupation and my protection. No more is this dark mountain a foreboding place; it is no longer the mountain of ridicule and humiliation. It has become the Mountain of Love, a place where we find Lover's Leap. I want to speak those words out to You, to tell You that I want to come away, to be with my Lover and to be like the gazelle or the young stag. I hear You say that I am the spice-laden mountain, and there are other spice-laden mountains.

"This is a dying place. A cross! Yours, Lord, and mine! I have to lay down my fears and inhibitions, put the masks and the protective armour down and dare to stand naked and vulnerable before You."

DAY 150

Song of Songs 8:14 (NASB)
Hurry, my beloved, and be like a gazelle or a young stag on the mountains of spices.

The final words are the Beloved's, and far from closing the story they open a life of exciting promise and adventure – the adventure of relationship. She knows already that this relationship is full of good things. She has listened hard and learned well, and from her state of destitution and depression anticipates fulfilment and abundance. There is no holding back. This will be no slow plod or arduous trek up the mountains; it will be full of abandon, wonder, delight and feasting. A young stag with all the fullness of youth, buoyant and ready to face all-comers, will leap from crag to crag with sure-footed ease. My mind leaps to Habakkuk:

Habakkuk 3:19
The Sovereign Lord is my strength; he makes my feet like the feet of a deer, he enables me to go to the heights.

Prayer & Contemplation:

"With the Beloved, I cry out to You, O Lover of my soul. And I know as surely as she does that I am changed forever. Whatever the future holds, I can face it confidently for I am eternally and unconditionally loved. Let's explore the heights. See you up there?"

Conclusion

John 14:2-4 (NIV)

In my Father's house there are many rooms, if it were not so, I would have told you. I am going there to prepare a place for you. And if I go and prepare a place for you, I will come back and take you to be with me that you also may be where I am. You know the way to the place where I am going...